THE STILL SMALL VOICE IN THE GAME OF LIFE

HOW TO DISCOVER GOD'S PLAN

Robert E. Joyce

The Still Small Voice in the Game of Life

Published by:
Christian International Publishing

P.O. Box 9000
Santa Rosa Beach, FL 32459
www.cipublishing.net

ISBN 978-0-9825942-1-6

TABLE OF CONTENTS

Acknowledgements   I

Chapter 1: Understanding the Prophetic   1

Chapter 2: Power of the Prophetic   11

Chapter 3: Our Prophetic Issues   23

Chapter 4: Fulfilling Your Destiny   33
                and Understanding Yourself

Chapter 5: Faith for the Prophet   41

Chapter 6: Apostolic Prophecy   55

Chapter 7: The Value of Prophetic Anointing   65

Chapter 8: Principles of the Prophetic   79

Chapter 9: Sun Stands Still   95

To My Wife LaVern

I am dedicating this book in memory of my late wife, Co-Pastor Laverne O. Joyce. Prophetess Laverne and I were married 25 years; we worked together as a Prophetic Team. She affirmed me by constantly speaking into my life as addressing me as a Mighty Man of God. She never allowed me to settle for anything short of God's best. She and I spent months fasting and praying to hear the voice of God, and activating the gifts of God in our lives. Her motivation provoked me to seek God to the point where God's presence and anointing is evident in my life today.

Unforgettable
Robert E. Joyce

ACKNOWLEDGEMENTS

I would like to give special thanks and appreciation to all those to whom I am indebted in the production of this book. Thanks to the Almighty God, for his inspiration, guidance, and Holy Spirit poured on me day and night. I could not accomplish anything without Him.

There are so many individuals who have invested in me and through our relationship has pulled the best out of me. I would like to acknowledge my and thank my Mother, the late Mrs. R.L. Fleming for her encouragement and wisdom. To my children, Quenton, Derrick, Starlette, Robert E. Joyce Jr., and Benjamin Joyce (I will always appreciate the love and support bestowed on me); To my Brothers, Pastor Michael Joyce and his wife Shirley, Harrison Joyce and his wife Katherine, thank you for being a rock of encouragement.

I give special dedication and acknowledgement to the late Prophet John Lattimore and the late Apostle Theodore Elder Herring, my first mentor whom planted and nurtured my gifts and calling.

I would like to extend special thanks and gratitude, to my Spiritual Father and Covering, The Honorable Dr. Bishop Bill Hamon and Mom Hamon of Christian International. Your Anointing and Prophetic experiences has enhanced and inspired me. Thanks for your teaching and covering; it has maximized my potential and made an incredible influence on my life. Special thanks to the C I Family of Churches.

Also, special thanks to Prophet Ron and Prophetess Anetria Wright (my armor bearers for many years). To my Pastoral Staff, Administrative Staff and Life Worship & Training Center Family, thanks for your labor of love and faithfulness. Special thanks to REJoyce Ministries Network and National Apostolic Prophetic School, of which have connected me with wonderful men and women of God....who have stamped me with the graces of God and stirred me to higher heights. Special thanks to my partners and long time friends, Bishop Michael Jones and his wife Co-Pastor Brenda, host of NAPS Prophetic Training School.

Special thanks to Apostle Chuck Clayton and wife Karen, Apostle Leon Walters and wife Donna; you've been stepping stones and have inspired, motivated and instrumental to birthing my success.

As Chaplain of the Detroit Pistons, I would like to thank Monica and Chucky Atkins, Grant and Tamia Hill, Lindsay and Ivy Hunter,

ACKNOWLEDGEMENTS

Ben and Shonda Wallace, Tayshaun Prince, Chauncey Billups, Rodney Stuckey and The Detroit Pistons Organization for blessing me and my family and ministry.

To all the people who have been a blessing to me whose names are not mentioned here, your reward awaits you in Heaven.

THE STILL SMALL VOICE IN THE GAME OF LIFE

Chapter 1
UNDERSTANDING THE PROPHETIC

There are principles concerning the prophetic that we need to know. Once we understand these principles, it is easier to hear from God, and to flow with what He wants to say to us.

PROPHETIC POINT
To understand the prophetic you MUST develop a solid relationship with God!

Before you were Born Again you were in Spiritual Darkness. In that Darkness there was peace, but when you became Born Again, the Light of God touched that Darkness and caused a disturbance!

When Light touches Darkness the Darkness has to flee, and Darkness doesn't want to flee and so there is conflict. You'll sense it within yourself. You and your flesh have been in control of your life, in Darkness, for years and now there's conflict between your Born Again Spirit and the Flesh, between Light and Darkness.

When you get saved the Light of the World takes up residence inside you, and you take this new Light back to your still-Dark home. Your family begins to war against you because you no longer represent the Darkness, the flesh, your old way of life.

At this point, the enemy starts releasing Principalities and Powers against you. Yet, we know that "no weapon formed against you will prosper."

The joy you once had while you were in darkness doesn't sit well anymore because Light is coming against it. But, in order to maintain that light, you need to increase your consumption of the Word of God!

PROPHETIC POINT
Only by eating the Word of the Lord will you have the spiritual strength necessary to wrestle against principalities of darkness.

> Now I Paul myself beseech you by the meekness and gentleness of Christ, who in presence [am] base among you, but being absent am bold toward you: **2 Corinthians 10:1**

> But I beseech [you] that I may not be bold when I am present with that confidence, wherewith I think

to be bold against some, which think of us as if we walked according to the flesh. **2 Corinthians 10:2**

For though we walk in the flesh, we do not war after the flesh: **2 Corinthians 10:3**

(For the weapons of our warfare [are] not carnal, but mighty through God to the pulling down of strong holds;) **2 Corinthians 10:4**

Casting down imaginations, and every high thing that exalteth itself against the knowledge of God, and bringing into captivity every thought to the obedience of Christ; **2 Corinthians 10:5**

It's easy to misunderstand spiritual truth when you are speaking to carnal understanding. It is the reason why you are afraid to share the Truth because there are people who will not understand you.

But there comes a boldness by the Holy Spirit that says you are going to say it no matter what people think! You think to yourself, "I'm going to say it even if it falls on unfertile ground." It's not the job of the sower (prophet) to cultivate the crop. You are just the mail carrier.

There is a saying, "Don't shoot the messenger." For believers, this means you must deliver the message of God, at all costs! I would rather be in trouble with the world than with God for not doing what He is telling me to do. If God is for you, that's more than the world against you!

Many churches mistakenly think that the congregation should not take on the characteristics of its pastor. But, how can this be so when the pastor is God's leader of that church, and God is an orderly God?

It is a compliment when the people of a church are unified under the vision God has given its leader ,so there is only one vision in a church house.

PROPHETIC POINT
When God plants you in a particular church, it is to gird up the vision of that House of God, not implement your own!

If you come there with that understanding, to help under gird God's vision for that house, He can work with you.

But, if you come with the intention to build your own vision, there will be division because you're breaking away from the delegated authority established there by God. And, if you continue, you'll be operating in rebellion which is a form of witchcraft.

Operating in rebellion will cause you to go to the "outhouse" with God where He will break you and place you back in line with the rest of His sheep. God has to whoop your little legs to get you back under the vision of that House.

4

PROPHETIC POINT
*We must avoid fighting the devil **in the flesh**!*

When we think of ways to retaliate, for example, "She said something about me, so I'm going to say something about her," or "He did this to me, so I'm going to do this to him," we're reacting out of the flesh instead of responding from the Spirit.

The devil is no match for you in the Spirit. And, you are no match for him when you're in the flesh! He wants to get you to fight him on his territory, where he'll win every time.

The difference between champions and non-champions is the ability to win on their own home court rather than on the enemy's court. Most professional teams have a winning record at home.

PROPHETIC POINT
Fighting the devil on God's Turf gives us "home court advantage."

When we do need to fight the devil, we must do it on God's turf with the, "weapons of our warfare that are not carnal, but mighty through God in pulling down strongholds to whoop the devil!" 2 Corinthians 10:4 – *Coach R.E. Joyce paraphrase!*

We are in a war, and we are not empty handed. We must utilize our spiritual weapons to properly defeat the enemy. One of the things happening to the church is that we are not using our weapons properly.

That means that we aren't turning our weapons on the enemy and consequently, we're having a crisis of "friendly fire." Friendly fire was a problem in Vietnam where our soldiers were shooting one another instead of the enemy.

When a church is not evangelistic in its vision or doesn't utilize its Gifts properly, it will begin to turn inward on itself and turn those Gifts of the Spirit on each other.

God gives us the Gift of Wisdom, the Word of Knowledge, Prophecy, and so on, to discern the workings of the devil and build up one another, not to misuse them and tear each other down. If you don't use the Gifts properly it becomes abnormal use.

Second Corinthians 10:5 tells us that we should be, "Casting down imaginations, and every high thing that exalts itself against the knowledge of God, and bringing into captivity every thought to the obedience of Christ."

The weapons that we are given are for the purpose of pulling down strongholds and defeating the enemy, not one another. The Word of God also tells us to, "Put on the whole armor of God that you may be able to stand against the wiles of the devil," Ephesians 6:11.

We know now that "wiles" means to lie and wait. That's what the devil does best; he lies and waits! "For we wrestle not against flesh and blood," Ephesians 6:12. Hell's army is organized and we need to be just as organized.

You can be a spiritual giant but if you are not properly organized you will not enjoy all of the blessings God has for you. Money will come in and it has to be directed into the correct channels to do the most good according to the vision God has given you.

PROPHETIC POINT
We must learn to have strategies, like Jesus, who was well organized, disciplined and efficient.

Many churches will not fulfill their destiny because they take a haphazard approach and have a chaotic situation. When people come you have to treat them with respect and place them in positions according to God's plan.

There must be organization in everything. God equips us for the Kingdom of God, and we must utilize those spiritual tools wisely. When hindrances, such as disorganization, rebellion, or distraction are removed, the will of God can flow freely.

The following scriptures illustrate this:

> Afterward they preached from town to town across the entire island until finally they reached Paphos, where they met a Jewish sorcerer, a false prophet named Bar-Jesus. **Acts 13:6**

He had attached himself to the governor, Sergius Paulus, a man of considerable insight and understanding. The governor invited Barnabas and Saul to visit him, for he wanted to hear the word of God. **Acts 13:7**

But Elymas, the sorcerer (as his name means in Greek), interfered and urged the governor to pay no attention to what Saul and Barnabas said. He was trying to turn the governor away from the Christian faith. **Acts 13:8**

Then Saul, also known as Paul, filled with the Holy Spirit, looked the sorcerer in the eye and said, "You son of the Devil, full of every sort of trickery and villainy, enemy of all that is good, will you never stop perverting the true ways of the Lord? **Acts 13:9-10**

And now the Lord has laid his hand of punishment upon you, and you will be stricken awhile with blindness." Instantly mist and darkness fell upon him, and he began wandering around begging for someone to take his hand and lead him. **Acts 13:11**

When the governor saw what had happened, he believed and was astonished at what he learned about the Lord. **Acts 13:12**

When the hindrance was removed, the governor was saved. Paul used a weapon of offense to have God remove the sorcerer because he was a hindrance to Sergius Paulus getting saved.

PROPHETIC POINT
When hindrances are removed, the will of God can flow freely, so Be Ready and Prepared to remove them!

PROPHETIC POINTS TO REMEMBER

- To understand the prophetic you must develop a solid relationship with God.
- To walk in God's Light you need to increase your consumption of the Word of God!
- When called to a particular church, you are to gird up the vision of that House, not implement your own!
- Avoid fighting the devil in the flesh by reacting, but rather respond from out the Spirit.
- Fight the devil - on God's turf - your home Court, with spiritual weapons, to pull down strongholds.
- Plan, organize and strategize like Jesus did. God equips us for the Kingdom of God and we must utilize those spiritual tools wisely.
- When hindrances are removed, the will of God can flow freely. Be ready, and willing to remove them!

Chapter 2
POWER OF THE PROPHETIC

The word "power" is referenced in the King James Version of the Bible 272 times! One of the ways God has given us power is through the use of the Prophetic Word which has the ability to move us out of our natural circumstances and into the realm of the supernatural.

The way to perfect this "power from on high" is by spending time in God's presence; praying, meditating, and worshipping Him. By doing this, you will minimize the distractions of the flesh and your own thoughts so that as Mark 13:11 says, when you prophesy "it is not you that speaks, but the Holy Ghost."

It's also vitally important for you to develop your own relationship with the Father. Don't try to emulate another man or woman's prophetic ministry. Get to know His voice so that you'll know *when* and *what* to prophesy. Respond to God the way He deals with you and only you!

PROPHETIC POINT
Developing a relationship with God takes spending time in His Word, in prayer and in worship.

A strong relationship with God will cause you to be certain of His leading, and increase the likelihood of your Prophecies being accurate. Our model of this is Jesus Christ, whose very name in both the Greek and Hebrew translation is "Anointed One."
Followers of Jesus are known as Christians, and in the game of life He is our Guard Man; both Point Guard and Shooting Guard, metaphorically.

For instance, the Shooting Guard ensures a high volume of shots by blocking the opposing team's moves to prevent them from scoring, while the Point Guard controls the ball and will pass it to his team's player who is in a position to shoot and score.

Our Guard Man, Jesus Christ, was the Second Adam, God in the flesh. Consequently, Jesus didn't use His 'God Power,' but rather operated in the Prophetic Anointing by the Holy Spirit.

He had access to the same Holy Ghost *Power* that we, as Born Again, Holy Spirit Baptized Believers have access to! But keep in mind that Jesus perfected that connection by spending many hours in prayer and worshipping God the Father.

Any action taken or word spoken that is dictated by the Holy Spirit produces two phenomena; Diagnosis and Prognosis. When a Word of Prophecy is uttered, the first step is to 'diagnose' the situation, the cause of the problem; then the person being prophesied to can relate to this diagnosis in order to have faith to hear the 'prognosis' or God's solution to the problem.

PROPHETIC POINT

Foretelling Words will produce a Current Diagnosis of the problem and a Future Prognosis or solution for that problem.

That's how Jesus operated and He's our example. Whenever you begin to move in the Holy Spirit, you will be equipped with power to function in the Prophetic. Always keep in mind the two part action of prophecy; Diagnosis and Prognosis.

At this time, I want to analyze the power of the Prophetic, which is actually the power within the Prophet. That power is the result of intimacy with God, the Father. It's the same intimacy that a Pastor experiences when counseling one of his sheep or congregation, and the same intimacy a Prophet feels when giving a predictive word to someone.

God's perfect will is for the Prophet to have empathy and concern for the one he is prophesying to. Likewise, a Pastor who ministers to his flock must be moved by love. The Bible says that when Jesus saw the multitudes He was "moved with compassion," Matthew 9:36.

PROPHETIC POINT

Intimacy with God will increase your compassion for others and willingness to be used by Him to answer their need.

A Word of Prophesy will possess both Current and Future characteristics. One of the things I try to do when I'm mentoring a Prophet is train them to give a Word that is in both the present *and* future tense.

The current Prophetic Word diagnoses one's situation (as we discussed earlier). A person can identify with the *current* Word, the diagnosis of their present circumstances. This will help to build up their faith to receive the Prophetic *future* Word, the prognosis and solution for their life and what they're going through.

In the next verses of scripture, we see a transformation in Nathaniel (also known as Bartholomew), whom Jesus called as a disciple. The prophetic Word Jesus spoke to him produced the revelation progression - past, present and future - in him.

Nathaniel and Phillip were close friends and immediately after Phillip answered Jesus' call to follow Him; he eagerly invited Nathaniel to go with him to where Jesus was staying and see for himself that Jesus was the Messiah.

Although Nathaniel was skeptical, *past tense*, he received Jesus' Word to him, *present tense*, and became, *future tense,* a true believer of Jesus Christ.

14

Jesus sees Nathanael coming to him, and saith of him, Behold an Israelite indeed, in whom is no guile! **John 1:47**

Nathanael saith unto him, Whence knowest thou me? Jesus answered and said unto him, Before that Philip called thee,
when thou wast under the fig tree, I saw thee. **John 1:48**

Nathanael answered and saith unto him, Rabbi, thou art the Son of God; thou art the King of Israel. **John 1:49**

Jesus answered and said unto him, Because I said unto thee, I saw thee under the fig tree, believest thou? Thou shalt see greater things than these. **John 1:50**

And he saith unto him, Verily, verily, I say unto you, Hereafter ye shall see heaven open, and the angels of God ascending and descending upon the Son of man. **John 1:51**

Jesus taught, "Man shall not live by bread alone, but by every Word that proceeds out of the mouth of God" Matthew 4:4. In this context, "proceeds" means 'continual.' It's not just one Word from God that we live on, but God's continual Words to us!

There should always be a Word from God for us because God never runs out of words, or anything for that matter! There's no lack in God! So, it's important that we continue to allow Him to speak to us and give us direction for our lives.

That's where the Old Testament was a type and shadow of the Shekinah Glory cloud which the Prophets followed. The Bedouins, desert dwellers who lived in tents, were able to quickly pick up and move where God told them in order to follow clouds heavy with rain.

Unlike you or I, they didn't have to worry about a home mortgage! When the Tent Dwellers heard the voice of God they could quickly uproot and follow Him. The important thing to remember is these Bedouins had a heart to follow God.

They could have stayed in their tents just like many of us stay in our 'comfort zone' tents because we don't want to uproot from the status quo. We need to develop a heart, and a willingness to go where God directs and speak what He instructs.

PROPHETIC POINT
We need to cultivate a Tent Dweller's heart, to be ready to leave life's comfortable rut and move with God where He says to go!

I remember old testimony services where people always talked about what God did "a long time ago." But no one can live off yesterday's Manna! We need a fresh Word from God. As Prophets, we need to have the confidence Elisha had when he told the King of Israel that he had the Word of the Lord inside him for that King!

> And it was [so], when Elisha the man of God had heard that the king of Israel had rent his clothes, that he sent to the king, saying, Wherefore hast thou rent thy clothes? Let him come now to me, and he shall know that there is a prophet in Israel. **2 Kings 5:8**

I believe, right now, that God can speak to me. You must also have that same assurance within you that God will speak a Word to you *for others*. It's a matter of stirring up the Gift.

If you don't believe me, believe Jesus! He didn't have an identity crisis. He boldly proclaimed, "I always do those things that please my Father", John 8:29. He also knew that God always heard His prayers. The Pharisees mistook Jesus' confidence for arrogance, and that hasn't changed!

You must get to the place where you can also say, "I am what I am by the grace of God" and make no apologies for being a Prophet. You didn't call yourself to be a Prophet. God did that when you were still in your mother's womb. So, you must have a Holy confidence in who you are and in who called you!

I believe there is this kind of Holy Ghost confidence that the Lord is restoring to the Church, much like Elisha had when he declared, "He (the King) shall know that there is a prophet in Israel."

17

You can paraphrase it like this, "The King will know that the Church is not dead! He'll know that God is alive and is living in me, Coach ReJoyce, the prophet!"

> And Elisha sent a messenger unto him, saying, Go and wash in Jordan seven times, and thy flesh shall come again to thee, and thou shalt be clean. **2 Kings 5:10**

Here we see the same illustration that is in the New Testament and that is the *power to heal* is in the Word. The prophetic Word has so much power that when we speak it, we release the supernatural power of God!

Let me say a quick word of admonition not to let prophetic Words from God be confused with a witch's words of the occult. They speak only information from a familiar spirit revelation, but only prophetic Words of God have the power to transform lives.

In everything we do prophetically, there is always an impartation of the Holy Ghost to break the powers of hell itself and bring transformation!

THE POWER OF AGREEMENT

> If two of you shall agree on earth as touching any
> thing that they shall ask, it shall be done for them of
> my Father which is in heaven. **Matthew 18:19**

Nothing is impossible if you find someone who will agree with
you. That's the Power of Agreement. For instance, if you are at
home praying about a car, "I have to have that car." Then, the
Word of the Lord comes to someone who has been praying in
agreement with you.

PROPHETIC POINT
*If Wilbur and Orville Wright had not exercised the Power of
Agreement, aviation might never have gotten off the ground!*

When they tell you that the car is on its way to you, you can rejoice
because the Power of Agreement produced a prophetic Word
concerning your situation.

> For thus saith the LORD God of Israel, The barrel of
> meal shall not waste, neither shall the cruse of oil fail,
> until the day [that] the LORD sendeth rain upon the
> earth. **1 Kings 17:14**

Notice that the prophetic Word had the Power of Provision. The
spoken prophetic Word creates and provides what is needed.
If you follow the entire story, you'll see that it's about the
relationship the Lord had with the prophet of God. Elijah knew

19

that whatever he said God would honor, because He honored their relationship.

It's similar to a husband and wife relationship. If my wife goes to the front desk of the church and orders something, they know that I'm going to pay for it. My wife can order anything she wants and they know that I'm going to cover it.

The relationship between you and God should be like good friends in that you don't meekly ask God if you might order this or that. No! You know that He will honor your request because of the relationship you both share.

God knows that He can depend on the Prophet not to ask anything that is contrary to His will. God and the Prophet are so linked that each knows the will of the other. They understand each other's authority over the natural realm.

> And he said, About this season, according to the time of life, thou shalt embrace a son. And she said, Nay, my lord, [thou] man of God, do not lie unto thine handmaid. **2 Kings 4:16**

> And the woman conceived, and bares a son at that season that Elisha had said unto her, according to the time of life.
> **2 Kings 4:17**

Elisha's prophetic Word had a baby in it! Here we see the creative words of the man of God caused life to come into that womb! The prophetic Word has that kind of creative power in it!

> So shall my word be that goeth forth out of my mouth: it shall not return unto me void, but it shall **accomplish** that which I please, and it shall prosper [in the thing] whereto I sent it. **Isaiah 55:11**

When you release a prophetic Word it will go and accomplish what it was sent to do. And remember, the prophetic Word is not from you or inspired by you. You're only delivering the mail, so to speak!

You and I should have no responsibility in making it come to pass. I don't care if it does or doesn't happen. I release myself from all of that. I only say and share prophetically what the Lord gives me. The prophetic Word, alone, has the power to bring it to pass.

> And the mother of the child said, [As] the LORD liveth, and [as] thy soul liveth, I will not leave thee. And he arose, and followed her. **2 Kings 4:30**

When God reveals to you the things you believe Him for, it causes you to move into agreement with God, not just acknowledgement of it. God's Word is true and has the power to do things beyond our imagination.

When you are in tune with His plan for you, the realization will come that it's in your best interest never to leave the Father's side. His love for you is so amazingly above anything you will ever see or know, that, why would you want to leave?

PROPHETIC POINTS TO REMEMBER

- Developing a relationship with God takes spending time in His Word, in prayer and in worship.
- Prophetic Words will produce a Current Diagnosis of a problem and a Future Prognosis or solution for that problem.
- Intimacy with God will increase your compassion for others and your willingness to be used to meet their need.
- We need to cultivate a Tent Dweller's heart, ready to leave our comfortable ruts and move where God says to go!
- If Wilbur and Orville Wright had not exercised the Power of Agreement, aviation might never have gotten off the ground!

Chapter 3
OUR PROPHETIC ISSUES

Now we will consider our image beyond our issues. These are our Prophetic Issues. Sometimes we have an issue about how we see ourselves. Sometimes we have to rename our situational issues in order to change our destiny.

When we go to the mirror we see different things and there is a big variance between what women and men see.

When a woman looks into the mirror she will see crow's eyes, wrinkles under her chin, and other such features she considers flaws. She probably feels bad about what she sees. On the other hand, when a man looks in the mirror and sees a bald head and a stomach hanging over his britches he thinks he's still "got it!"

But a mirror only reflects a physical image. What God sees and is concerned with is what's inside us, our spiritual image. It is important that we have a correct image of who we are spiritually, as well as physically.

Let's look at Genesis 1:26-28.

> And God said, Let us make man in our image, after our likeness: and let them have dominion over the fish of the sea, and over the fowl of the air, and over the cattle, and over all the earth, and over every creeping thing that creepeth upon the earth. **Genesis 1:26**

> So God created man in his [own] image, in the image of God created he him; male and female created he them. **Genesis 1:27**

> And God blessed them, and God said unto them, Be fruitful, and multiply, and replenish the earth, and subdue it: and have dominion over the fish of the sea, and over the fowl of the air, and over every living thing that moveth upon the earth. **Genesis 1:28**

This chapter will be a reflection of the Power of the Prophetic, relative to helping us in the area of our image. Mankind is made in the image of God. The Bible tells us that the man is the head of the home.

For the husband is the head of the wife, even as Christ
is the head of the church: and he is the saviour of the
body. **Ephesians 5:23**

As the head of the home, God intends man to be a reflection
of Christ, who is the head of man. If a man is mirroring God
correctly to his wife, the light that reflects off him will touch his
wife, and she will reflect the light of God that's in her husband
to her children. Lastly, her children will reflect that same godly
image to those around them.

That's God's image for a family's household. This is why
behavior is so important. When sin entered the earth we began to
see and hear things that affected us negatively. One of the ways
men are affected is through the eye-gate.

For example, the devil will deceive young and older men alike
into believing distorted things as though they were true. These
distorted images often come through words, whether from
family, friends, bosses or even pastors.
Think of some of the things you have heard as a child, those
"nicknames," Stinky, Blackie, Dummy, Fatso, Four Eyes! Those
names effect and distort self images. It is imperative that if
someone planted that kind of seed in you that it be uprooted. If
not, that bad seed will grow.

There is an idea that was popular several years ago called "self-
fulfilling prophecy." People would call you something, you

would see yourself that way and then, you would fulfill it, or act accordingly so that it was fulfilled.

If they said you were never going to be anything, then, even if you reached a measure of success in your life you would still feel like a failure. Consequently, you would find a way to abort your success because you felt unworthy of success.

With the negative and destructive issues so many of us live with, we can begin to understand how powerful the prophetic can be to realign us in our thinking and actions.

If you want to change your behavior there are three things you need to know.

PROPHETIC POINT
One : *Whatever goes in your mind affects your thinking.*

That's why the devil has taken so many young peoples' minds captive with songs. Song lyrics affect the way they think. When a song says profane and negative things about women, then, the value of women depreciates in the mind of the listener.

PROPHETIC POINT
Two: *Whatever you think affects your actions and performance.*

If your thinking becomes distorted and you feel unworthy of good relationships or success, you will do things that aren't in your best interest; you might start smoking, doing drugs or drinking on the job. Ultimately, these bad habits will attract bad things to you and repel the good.

PROPHETIC POINT

Three: *Your actions and performance affects your future.*

It's important that you have a correct image of yourself. Your environment can cause you to have the wrong image about yourself. As a Prophet you have to manifest the things of God, if you do not, people will not come to you when they need help from God.

Here's a simple rule to remember;

> ➤ *Your Thoughts determine your Actions.*
> ➤ *Actions determine your Habits.*
> ➤ *Habits determine your Character.*
> ➤ *Character determines your Destiny.*

Heredity also plays an important role in your behavior and the way you approach life. Your parents and grandparents are where your behavior stems from. If you can remember things that happened to you before you were 7 years old, good or bad, it probably was significant.

Psychologists say that the core being of a person is developed by the time they are 7 years old. Fearfulness, courage, cleanliness, or sloppiness are qualities we are instilled with from childhood.

When I was growing up, dirty dishes in the sink were not tolerated, therefore, when I was looking for a wife I was looking for a companion who valued cleanliness and good hygiene as much as I did.

Because of that, I wanted to see the environment she lived under. If there were roaches in her house, then, she probably wasn't the woman for me!

When these products of your behavior are considered, they affect the image that you have of yourself. The voice of the Lord will scatter the enemies of your soul, which are made up of your mind, will and emotions.

You were meant to function successfully in life and the prophetic Word has the ability to read your DNA. By that, I mean that when the Prophetic ministry begins to go forth to someone, we begin to pull out their DNA and look at not the way they are functioning, but how they were designed to function

It's almost like an Operator's Manual. At Christmas, most men will not read the Operator's Manual when trying to put together a new toy or tool...until something goes wrong! Then, they go and read the manual.

The Prophetic pulls out your Manual and reads the very fiber of your being. That's why when a Prophet taps into the core of your being they can tell you things about yourself that even you didn't know!

I know that a lot of people say that the prophetic is only confirmation. Those are the people who do not know what they are talking about. I know people who have prophesied things to me that I did not have a clue about, and I'm a prophet of God. We learned in chapter 2 that the Word of prophecy is Current and Future.

I will never forget the time when we were trying to purchase a building, and we believed God for that building. When the deal didn't go through I was ready to give up my position as a Prophet. A woman named Joyce Haden came, and said that the Lord wanted me to know that I didn't miss God, that it was only a Divine delay.

It was a delay sent by God purposefully, then, Leon Walters told me that God had no intention of giving us that building. It was a test of faith. The building we were looking at didn't stretch our faith enough! Its faith level was too low!

The building that we have now is twice the monthly financial obligation of that first building. Because of that test, I have faith to believe God on a higher level. God was stretching our faith, and I had no idea that that's what He wanted to do with me.

Those two Prophets pulled my DNA and prophesied what God was saying. My DNA was to believe God for bigger things than my mind thought! As a man thinks in his heart, so is he, Proverbs 23:7 says. If you want to change a man's behavior you have to change the way he thinks.

Now, if you will turn to 1 Kings with me I want to show you how a man was called a nickname and did not accept it.

We were talking about nicknames previously and here is a biblical illustration of that.

> And it came to pass, when Ahab saw Elijah, that Ahab said unto him, [Art] thou he that troubleth Israel? **Kings 18:17**

> And he answered, I have not troubled Israel; but thou, and thy father's house, in that ye have forsaken the commandments of the LORD, and thou hast followed Baalim. **1 Kings 17-18 1**

We see here that Elijah would not concede to being the trouble of Israel. He didn't see himself as a "troublemaker." One of the things that happens is we accept what other people say about us and submit to the way it makes us feel, which is usually bad. It's important not to allow people to put you in a box.

Jeremiah 1:5 tells us that, "Before I formed thee in the belly I knew thee; and before thou camest forth out of the womb I sanctified thee, [and] I ordained thee a prophet unto the nations." God knew you before you were formed, before you knew which way was up, God knew you!

God put a sense of destiny into your heart. Jeremiah made the mistake of trying to tell God why he wouldn't be an ideal

Prophet. He was too young and inadequate to speak for God. But God knew Jeremiah's DNA!

> But the LORD said unto me, Say not, I [am] a child: for thou shalt go to all that I shall send thee, and whatsoever I command thee thou shalt speak. **Jeremiah 1:7**

> Be not afraid of their faces: for I [am] with thee to deliver thee, saith the LORD. **Jeremiah 1:8**

> Then the LORD put forth his hand, and touched my mouth. And the LORD said unto me, Behold, I have put my words in thy mouth. **Jeremiah 1:9**

Notice that God did not ask him but He commanded him. There are some words, as a Prophet, that we are commanded to speak. Sometimes prophetically we are given our own free will. We do not have to speak unless we want to speak. However, there are those times when we are commanded to articulate what God lays on our hearts to say.

During those times when you are hesitant to speak out what God is telling you, just remember what God told Jeremiah in chapter one, verse eight; "Be not afraid of their faces, for I am with thee to deliver thee."

PROPHETIC POINTS TO REMEMBER

- Whatever goes in your mind affects your Thinking.
- Whatever you think affects your Actions.
- Your actions and performance affects your future.

> ➤ *Your Thoughts determine your Actions.*
> ➤ *Actions determine your Habits.*
> ➤ *Habits determine your Character.*
> ➤ *Character determines your Destiny.*

Chapter 4
FULFILLING YOUR DESTINY
... AND UNDERSTANDING YOURSELF

The time is now to let the Prophets rise! Look at the Book of Judges, chapter 14 because one of the things I have found in the Body of Christ is that if we are going to fulfill our Destiny we must understand ourselves.

One of the things we do in our Marriage Seminars is biblical Personality Profiles. The idea is that if I can understand me, then, I can understand you. If I understand myself, then, I will be able to properly relate and interact with other people.

In the Body of Christ if I understand my Gifting, my ability, then, I will find myself far more successful in the things of God. An example is and some people get upset with this example, in our natural body we have to wash it.

Not only do we have to wash it, we have to pay more attention to certain parts of the body. These are parts of the body that need a little more care than the others. I can always tell when those parts are not getting the attention they need (and sometimes so can others!).

Just like our natural body, in the Body of Christ there are members who need more attention also. God gives us pastors who are anointed to pay attention to the not so fresh parts of the Body of Christ.

Another point is that to know yourself you have to make sure you are not copying anyone else. If God wanted two of one individual He would have made two of them and none of you. So, He made you uniquely yourself.

God loves variety. God brings diversity. In the Body of Christ we often make the mistake of focusing on our differences in the negative instead of focusing on them in the positive, the way God does.

It is our differences that create unique and distinct assignments in the Body of Christ. Look at the diversity of the prophets. Not one prophet was given the full revelation. I don't care how smart you think you are; you are only one piece of the puzzle.

PROPHETIC POINT

If you feel like you don't fit in, it may be that God wants to use your special talent in ways no one else could, except you!

No one prophet had the full revelation of God. Look at Isaiah who had the revelation of a Holy God. When he looked up to God as, "Holy, Holy, Holy!"

When you listen to certain preachers all they talk about is holiness. Don't get upset because all they talk about is holiness, that's where their revelation is. That's where their insight is, where their vision is. Where they can get into error is when they try to take their revelation and put it on everyone else.

If you look at Hosea, he only spoke of a wounded, loving God. He always talked about God being rejected yet loving. Hosea fell in love with and married a prostitute. Every time she left him for another man, Hosea searched for her, found her and brought her back to care for her.

Hosea's marital life reflected the "adulterous" relationship which Israel had built in going after and serving other gods. Even though his wife abandoned him, as Israel had abandoned God, Hosea took her back, just as God forgave and took Israel back.

That's why Hosea spoke of a rejected, loving God. Every time he would talk about God he talked about God being rejected yet forgiving.

When we look at Amos, we see how he passionately called for social justice. He was a type of Martin Luther King. He was deeply troubled by the social injustices and material disparities that existed.

When he talked of God his message was of God's desire for social justice and righteousness to prevail.

Jeremiah's revelation was of God's continual judgment. He kept saying, almost like Flip Wilson, that "God's gonna getcha for that!" Every time you saw him he was saying, "Y'all better straighten up."

Jeremiah is sometimes referred to as the "weeping prophet" because of his pleadings for Israel to repent and escape God's judgment.

Ezekiel's one prevailing thought was of a coming restoration when the Israelites would return to their own land and rebuild their kingdom. God's glory would return, and would be greater in the latter house than it was in the former house.

Ezekiel's vision is an allegory of the relationship between the Church and God. We, as members of the Body of Christ, are encouraged in the area of restoration. The Book of Ezekiel shows a clear pattern that we need to follow.

~~~~~~~~~~

One of the things that God is establishing in the Body of Christ is the Gift of Discerning of Spirits. In this way, we can discern the originator of things, to know who is causing us to do what we do. What is present in the church, or in my home and environment?

There are four basic types of spirits. There is 1) the spirit of God, 2) the spirit of the devil, 3) there is your spirit and 3) there are angelic spirit beings. The Gift of Discerning Spirits causes us to understand who it is that is giving us our motivation.

PROPHETIC POINT
The best way to know what is behind a situation you're facing is to ask the Holy Spirit to reveal it to you.

Now with Samson, God's purpose for him was not to have a beautiful physique. God's purpose was that he might destroy the enemies of Israel. Instead of doing that, Samson got sidetracked and deceived by Delilah.

After he had been reduced to a defeated man, blinded and harnessed like an animal, Samson cried out to God to give him strength to use his Gift and fulfill God's purpose one final time.

He pulled down the massive pillars holding up the temple where all the leaders of the Philistines were gathered. Down came the temple on the rulers, all the people and on himself. Judges 16:30 says that Samson "killed many more as he died, than while he lived."

God sometimes called us to stand in intercession against the power of drugs. But we won't because we'd rather look at television, until something happens that shakes us out of our stupor.

When someone in your family gets hooked on drugs, and breaks into your house looking for money to buy more drugs with, that's when all of a sudden, you become a prayer warrior which was God's purpose for us all along!

Another example is, in some cases, God calls us to pray for husbands. But because you have a nice loving husband, you do not think you have to pray.

Then, one day the devil gets on him and he hits you. Now all of a sudden you become a prayer warrior for your husband.

What I'm saying to you is that we must understand God's purpose and assignment for us so that God won't have to do some things to get our attention.

God shook the entire ocean to get Jonah's attention, caused a whale to swallow him up. Ask yourself, right now, "Am I being obedient to God or is God looking for me and sending a whale my way?"

God will put you in situations where there is no pressure to perform, to see if you will perform. Don't make Him put the pressure on you!

> For we dare not make ourselves of the number, or compare ourselves with some that commend themselves: but they measuring themselves by themselves, and comparing themselves among themselves, are not wise. **2 Corinthians 10:12**

> But we will not boast of things without [our] measure, but according to the measure of the rule which God

hath distributed to us, a measure to reach even unto you. **2 Corinthians 10:13**

Paul understood his measure of authority. He was determined not to go beyond that measure of rule. It's only when you go beyond your degree of authority that you get yourself in trouble, or you begin to get embarrassed.

In the things of God, we have to understand the measure of rule or authority God has given us. That determines where He has given us an anointing. My definition of anointing is simply this:

➢ *The anointing is the ability of God to perform a task.*

Whatever task God has called you to do He has equipped you supernaturally to perform that task. Now, if you are performing a task that He hasn't equipped you to do, then, you are operating out of one of two types of powers.

One is soul powers, which are your mind, will and emotions. The other power is physical power which also includes force of character.

In order to be successful spiritually, it is necessary to understand where our anointing is, and where our measure of rule starts and ends.

PROPHETIC POINT

The weapons of our spiritual warfare are made to fit our own exact specifications. No one else's weapons or anointing will do.

We all start out as sheep, but you might have a call on your life to become a Shepherd. The only one who can transform a sheep into a shepherd is God.

If you do not wait to receive the anointing, then it results in sheep leading other sheep. The feat of transforming a sheep into a Shepherd hasn't taken place.

In order for you to be transformed and fulfill your destiny, you must know your measure of rule and this must be understood and actively practiced. Only then will you fulfill your destiny!

PROPHETIC POINTS TO REMEMBER

- If you feel like you don't fit in, it may be that God wants to use your special talent in ways no one else could, except you!
- The best way to know what is behind a situation you're facing is to ask the Holy Spirit to reveal it to you.
- The weapons of your spiritual warfare are made to fit your own exact specifications. No one else's weapons *or anointing* will do.

Chapter 5
FAITH FOR THE PROPHET

The Bible says that faith comes by hearing, and hearing by the Word of God. Whatever we preach, we have an obligation to allow God to confirm the Word.

In our Conferences and Seminars, we try to assemble various groups of individuals to bring us distinctive prophetic anointings. Prophets have the ability to bring different aspects of God.

I want to continue where we left off in chapter 4. We were discussing the different revelations of some of the important prophets in the Bible. First, let's review.

When Isaiah saw God he saw Him as a holy God. After he saw God, and then, saw himself, he exclaimed, "I am a man of unclean lips!"

Then said I, Woe [is] me! for I am undone; because I [am] a man of **unclean lips**, and I dwell in the midst of a people of **unclean lips**: for mine eyes have seen the King, the LORD of hosts. **Isaiah 6:5**

That was his revelation of God. Jeremiah's revelation was that God was a God of judgment. Every time Jeremiah spoke of God he'd say, "God is going to get your butt!" (paraphrase).

He always talked about the judgment of God. Amos's revelation was of a God who was against social injustice. That was his insight. Hosea had a revelation of a wounded and rejected, yet forgiving and loving God. Hosea saw Him as one who might say, "I would rather have loved and lost than never have loved at all" (paraphrase).

> ➢ *'Tis better to have loved and lost,*
> *Than never to have loved at all.*

      ---Lord Alfred Tennyson, *In Memoriam*, 1850

Hosea perceived that God wanted to show you how to really love. God told him to go and marry a woman, a harlot, who would leave Hosea to be with another man. Then, God wanted Hosea to take care of her new boyfriend, as well!

Isaiah, Jeremiah, Amos, Elijah, Elisha, and Ezekiel all had a different revelation of God.

PROPHETIC POINT

The weapons of our spiritual warfare are made to fit our own exact specifications. No one else's weapons or anointing will do.

The Bible says that when King Saul came among the prophets that he was transformed into another man. This account is very interesting because Saul had intended to have David captured in order to kill him by sending out his warriors to bring him in.

However, when the warriors came into David's presence, who was surrounded by Samuel and the other prophets, the warriors also began to prophesy. When Saul heard what happened, he sent more troops to capture David, but the same thing happened!

Finally, Saul set out himself to go and get David, but when Saul came under the umbrella of the company of all those prophets he had a radical transformation! He took his clothes off and for 24 hours he prophesied the Word of the Lord. He prophesied so much that the other prophets asked, "Is Saul also among the Prophets?"

> And **Saul** sent messengers to take David: and when they saw the company of the prophets prophesying, and Samuel standing [as] appointed over them, the Spirit of God was upon the messengers of **Saul**, and they also prophesied. **1 Samuel 19:20**

> And when it was told **Saul**, he sent other messengers, and they prophesied likewise. And **Saul** sent messengers again the third time, and they prophesied also. **1 Samuel 19:21**

> And he stripped off his clothes also, and prophesied before Samuel in like manner, and lay down naked all that day and all that night. Wherefore they say, [Is] **Saul** also among the prophets? **1 Samuel 19:24**

Saul left there with a new title. When you come up under that umbrella, faith is released into the atmosphere so that your gifts are multiplied.

Not only that, when the prophetic anointing is released people will prophesy whether they believe in it or not. God still bypasses your mind and deals with your heart.

PROPHETIC POINT

A Paradigm Shift is a fundamental change in belief, attitude or way of doing things.

The Church is undergoing a paradigm shift, changing its belief and approach brought about by the fusing together of the Apostolic and the Prophetic anointing.

> Therefore leaving the principles of the doctrine of Christ, let us go on unto perfection; not laying again the foundation of repentance from dead works, and of faith toward God. **Hebrews 6:1**

We will obtain Apostolic insight of what we see God is doing. The next scripture is what I want to use as a text.

Wherefore I will not be negligent to put you always in remembrance of these things, though ye know [them], and be established in the present truth. **2 Peter 1:12**

There are some things that God will do in the future, but "present truth" means this is what God is doing in the earth, right now.

It's amazing when you visit various churches, if you're tuned in, you will discover how certain songs will cause that house of God to rise up! For that particular season, singing those particular songs will bring the power of God in.

Then, when that season has passed that song no longer has the same effect that it once had. The song's season is also over. It is crucially important that the Music Ministry understands what God is saying and doing at a certain time for a particular church. Otherwise, they will continue living and worshiping on stale revelation Manna!

The same thing is true in the Word of God. We have to know what God is saying and doing at this hour and at this season so that we may stay continuously connected with God. Only in this way can we fight the good fight of faith, and be established in the present truth that God is moving in, on the earth, now.

One of the things that I have the responsibility of doing is laying a solid foundation for Christ, and making sure that you have a solid foundation. Sometimes churches are the only group of people who are not willing to start with the basics. They seem to always want to bypass that goal and jump immediately into the deep waters of God.

PROPHETIC POINT
The degree of success you have in Ministry and in life will be determined by the foundation you build on, firm or flimsy.

As a result, they become imbalanced. That's why it's imperative that we endeavor to lay a solid foundation. That solid foundation includes a responsibility to not only preach salvation but to also move into the dimension of Kingdom living.

A lot of preachers only preach salvation, which is excellent, but Kingdom living must be a part of it also. Kingdom living is the area where we begin to dominate, to seize the atmosphere, and to control the elements around us.

The Prophet is not going to speak bubblegum Words like, "God is about to bless you." That's fine, but God wants you to step up to a higher level. He wants you to proclaim on Earth what God is saying in the Heavens.

> So the priests, and the Levites, and the porters, and the singers, and [some] of the people, and the Nethinims, and all Israel, dwelt in their cities; and when the seventh month came, the children of Israel [were] in their cities. **Nehemiah 7:73**

God is, now, in a place where He is breaking out of traditional boundaries in the Church. A "paradigm shift" can be described as a major change in our set mental thought patterns – a drastic shift in our personal beliefs that affects our life responses and all behavior patterns.

God is breaking down these patterns. He's changing it and the Church needs to be aware of how He's doing it. Some theologians would call this Advanced Decision Making. It is essentially, the way we think and process data, so we can make effective decisions when necessary. Well, God is breaking up and transforming those thought patterns and old ways of doing things!

> And, be not conformed to this world: but be ye transformed by the renewing of your mind, that ye may prove what [is] that good, and acceptable, and perfect, will of God.
> **Romans 12:1**

There is a renewing of the mind, a brainwashing, so to speak. You need to be reprogrammed in your thinking. The Word of God has the ability to wash our brains, so we will conform to the Word of God and not to the world or to traditions. God is manifesting new things.

> Thou hast heard, see all this; and will not ye declare [it]? I have shewed thee new things from this time,

even hidden things, and thou didst not know them. **Isaiah 48:6**

They are created now, and not from the beginning; even before the day when thou heardest them not; lest thou shouldest say, Behold, I knew them. **Isaiah 48:7**

This is a season and time when God is unveiling new things to us. He is beginning to unveil, reveal and manifest Himself, first in the natural, and then in the spiritual. This is not limited to revivals, which is bringing back or reviving what we've already had.

This is a complete reformation and transformation of the Church. The word 'reformation' means to make a structural adjustment; to make straight that which was broken or protrudes or is misshapen.

Now when these things were thus ordained, the priests went always into the first tabernacle, accomplishing the service [of God]. **Hebrews 9:6**

It's time for the church to be reformed. The world outside is looking for a specific theme to a church, but we are no longer doing that specific thing, and the world isn't able to find what it's looking for. That's why we're not having any effect on the world.

For instance, Jesus said, "By this shall all men know that you are my disciples, if you have love one to another," John 13:35. The question of the hour is, "Do we all love one another?"

We don't love one another when we get on the phone and talk ugly about each other or against other preachers. We waste God's holy time talking negative about preachers. Then, you wonder why God isn't honoring your words. He can't honor that because it is out of order, and in strife.

James 3:16 says, "For where envying and strife is, there is confusion and every evil work." God isn't about to honor that!

So, God has to deal with us on the inside. We need God to show us His fire. We need the Refiner's fire to come into the Church. You'll stop all that foolishness when you start feeling the fire of God! When you get under His fire you don't have time to worry about what anyone else is doing, let alone talk ugly about it!

PROPHETIC POINT

A refining fire is used to bring metals, sugar and petroleum to a top quality state, free from impurities. God's fire will do the same thing in us!

Remember how immediately after 9/11 the Church started getting along? Pastors, who I didn't know but who knew me, asked me to come and speak to their congregations. I thought those people did not like preachers from our parts. But they wanted someone to get a prayer through because their sons and daughters were going overseas as soldiers to fight.

So, I'm telling you, what God is doing is bringing His fire because that fire will cause you to be purified on the inside. He's causing His wind to blow away all the impurities.

God is totally and profoundly redesigning the outer manifestations of the Church in the earth by means of a deep interchange or exchange within the Body of Christ.

> And they found written in the law which the LORD had commanded by Moses, that the children of Israel should dwell in booths in the feast of the seventh month.
> **Nehemiah 8:14**

> And when the seventh month was come, and the children of Israel [were] in the cities, the people gathered themselves together as one man to Jerusalem.
> **Ezra 3:1**

The seventh month was a time of new Light as referenced in the Books of Nehemiah and Ezra. In this Age, God is sovereignly fulfilling His purpose, through the spoken words of the Prophets, which is to bring His Church to its ultimate destiny.

When the prophetic Word comes and God's people act on it, you move into the dimension of Apostolic Reformation. That is what God is moving the church into. We must do what He says, and finish the work by staying the course. That's what the Apostolic Movement is all about.

PROPHETIC POINT

Covenants are sealed agreements used socially, in business, government, and in our legal system. The first Covenant was between God and Noah, sealed by a rainbow.

The Church has gone through several different transformations because of Covenants to get to where we are now. These include the Abrahamic, Davidic, Mosaic, Salt and Circumcision Covenants.

Genesis 12:2 tells us that in the Abrahamic Covenant God promised to make the descendants of Abraham a great nation so that all the people on earth would be blessed through Abraham. Then, there was simply a Salt Covenant. Salt represents preservation, commitment, loyalty, purity, faithfulness and obedience. The mingling of salt in the Covenant of Salt signified an everlasting relationship between two parties, namely, God and man. I want you to always remember that you are in Covenant with God.

Another Covenant was Circumcision. It's interesting that women were left out of this. And, all the women can say, Praise the Lord! Then we moved on! We moved into the laws of God, known as the Mosaic Covenant.

The Davidic Covenant established David and his descendants as the rightful kings of Judah which was important relative to Jesus being of the lineage of David.

51

Then, we moved over into a time when John the Baptist came on the scene and told everyone that what they had to do was repent and be baptized.

Through Jesus, in the New Testament, the New Covenant was established. At the Last Supper, Jesus took "the cup of the New Covenant" and declared that the Old Testament law was fulfilled in Him. Through Him the sins of the world would be taken away.

Jesus died, and now He is resurrected, and tells everybody who watched this transformation that you not only need to be baptized in the name of Jesus for the remission of sins, but also to be baptized and filled with the Holy Ghost.

There were some individuals who made every transition, but there were some who did not. Some stayed stuck back in the laws of Moses. It's best not to get stuck in what God has already done. Praise and worship Him for it, but move on with Him.

Praise God for what He has done, praise and worship Him for what He is doing now. Be an active participant in what He is now doing and is going to do in the future. God is not governed by time constraints, so don't you be either!

PROPHETIC POINTS TO REMEMBER

- Just as there many different types of personalities, there are many Revelations various individuals will have to reveal their own perspective of God.
- A Paradigm Shift is a fundamental change in belief, attitude or way of doing things.
- What you do in Ministry, and what you accomplish in life will only be as successful as the foundation you build on, firm or flimsy.
- A refining fire is used to bring metals, sugar and petroleum to a top quality state, free from impurities. God's fire will do the same thing in us!
- Covenants are sealed agreements used socially, in business, government, and in our legal system. The first Covenant was between God and Noah, sealed by a rainbow.

Chapter 6
APOSTOLIC PROPHESY

I believe that we need to learn to enjoy God. I want to enjoy God because he says you are not going to only have life, but you are going to have it more abundantly.

When I used to fight there was nothing greater for me than to start laughing at my opponent. It stole his confidence. That's why when we begin to laugh at the devil it causes him to go and find someone else.

The prophetic is more than just a word; it is the restoration of all the Gifts. God is not coming back for a half dressed woman. No one wants a raggedy bride. So the Church has to be fully dressed, without spot or blemish, in order for the groom to come back.

How many of us know that the job of the bride is to please the groom? The responsibility of the bride on the night that the marriage is consummated is to please him. When we are worshiping God we don't need to leave worship until He is pleased. At the same time, we should not stop preaching until God is satisfied.

We should not stop giving until God is pleased. It is important for Prophetic people, who are hearing the Word of God, to be hearers and doers of the Word of God. Blessed are they that hear the Word of God and keep it.

PROPHETIC POINT
The Apostle Paul first used the phrase, 'Meat Head' in Romans 8:6, "to be carnally minded is death." The word carnal comes from the root carne for meat and head represents the mind. So, Paul is telling us, "Don't be a meat head!"

When we hear the Word of God we have a responsibility to adhere to it. Why should God keep talking to you when you're not doing what He has already stated?

What are some of the prayers that you have asked God for and He did not answer? Maybe he said to Gabriel, "Don't pay attention to that!" Maybe the reason is because you have bickering and back biting in your home or church.

There is a restoration of relationships that is taking place in our lives. There is a restoration of a Heavenly or Divine view of things. What happened in some previous generations is that we would devise our own plans and agendas, and then go to God and ask Him to bless them. And sometimes He would and sometimes he wouldn't. However, now with the Prophetic Divine viewpoint we receive the mind of God, act on it and it is already blessed. How many of us know that He is the author and a finisher of our faith?

He is responsible to bring in the equipment. He is responsible to bring in the people and to bring in the money. I tell everybody everywhere I go not to worry about the budget.

The good news is that the finances are there; the bad news is that the finances are in your pocket! Loosen yourself and let it go free.

For though ye have ten thousand instructors in Christ, yet [have ye] not many fathers: for in Christ Jesus I have begotten you through the gospel. **1 Corinthians 4:15**

In this chapter we are going to talk about calling forth fathers. The prophetic will point us toward the Apostolic.
I want to give you just a glance of one of the dimensions of the Apostolic relative to the Prophetic. We will bring clarity to you, the follower of Christ, that shall begin to emerge in your life.

When Paul was preaching in Corinth, he was dealing with misconceptions about his ministry. There were a lot of misunderstandings about his Apostolic ministry, so he took great time in helping people to understand and clear up any misgivings concerning his ministry.

In order to begin to understand the Apostle we must begin with the information that we have. We'll begin with a view from Malachi 4:6.

> And he shall turn the heart of the fathers to the children, and the heart of the children to their fathers, lest I come and smite the earth with a curse.
> **Malachi 4:6**

Here, God speaks very accurately about relationships. Relations must start from the heart and not the head. There are people who will come into your life only temporarily, but there are some people that God will put in your life forever.

We need to understand that God is interested in relationships. God is going to begin to deal with us according to our attitudes about the relationships He has placed in our lives.

The devil assumes the spirit of abortion to try and abort or terminate relationships that God has placed in your life. The enemy will try to make you mad at people God has put in your path to strategically help you.

Proverbs 27:17 says, "Iron sharpens iron." Whenever you ask God to take you to the next level, He will send someone in your life who will help you get to that next stage.

PROPHETIC POINT

The most important relationships in our lives are often those that profoundly changed us and made a difference in our lives.

Do you know that when iron sharpens iron sparks fly into the atmosphere? Most of us have been hurt before, and often we run away from the relationship instead of allowing God to deal with us in our attitudes toward it.

There are some people who will come into your life that you instantly begin to pray about. God would allow certain people to come into your life that will cause you to pray. We must learn not to be promiscuous, in the sense that rather than work at a relationship, we just go get another one.

Before Jesus got on the Main Line with us our pattern of behavior would be to get into relationship, and soon, break up with them when they find out that we weren't who and what we said we were. So, we went to someone else who didn't know how we were.

That behavior carried right on into church. We would go to a church where they didn't know what we were about and we'd start all over again. But, then some of the folks at the new church would find out that we weren't who and what we said we were, and off we'd go to another church. And so on, and so on.

Apostolic fathers will be very strong in relationship, while Satan hates relationships because of the power in agreement. Deuteronomy 32:30 says that, "One can chase a thousand, and two can put 10,000 to flight." So, the enemy hates God ordained relationships.

You must understand when anybody comes into your life there are only four ways they will impact you. They will add, subtract, multiply or divide you and what's yours.

Ask someone, what are you doing in my life? There are three types of relationships that Apostolic fathers should have and those are, 1) as a mentor, 2) as a protégé, 3) and as a friend.

Mentoring is a partnership relationship. It is a junior partner with a senior partner. The purpose of this relationship is for progress. In order for this relationship to be successful the junior partner must be coachable.

It's amazing how many people are not coachable. You must be faithful, you must be available, and you must be teachable. As a junior partner, you don't know anything.

There is a relationship that I was in one time with someone I knew that God was working on. To me, they seemed to think they knew everything. Sometimes I will walk up to people like that and say, 'Hey, how are you doing, God?' since they acted like they knew everything.

Regardless of how much you know there's always a lot more that you don't know. The average person only uses between 7 to 10% of their brain, which means there's a whole lot of stuff up there that you are not using! So, it's very important that we remain teachable, especially when you find yourself in an environment where people want to teach you.

A mentor must be able to speak into your life, and you must be able to receive it. They may become the number one stress point in your life because they won't accept you the way you are. They see the expected end for you and want to see you get there. They see your ability and your talents. They see where you are. They see where you need to be going, so they can give you guidance for your life.

You can have more than one mentor, because one may be good in one area but not good in another. You must be able to discern someone else's motives before allowing them to mentor you in another area. But true mentors are very strong role models.

One that ruleth well his own house, having his children in subjection with all gravity. **1 Timothy 3:4**

It is necessary to see that a true mentor will have things in order. We need to look for someone to be a John the Baptist for us, but we also need to be a John the Baptist for somebody else. That is the forerunner to opening the door for someone else.

And when Jesus was entered into Capernaum, there came unto him a centurion, beseeching him. **Matthew 8:5**

Notice in the above scripture that in order for the Mentoring relationship to function properly you must be under authority; if you're not under authority God will not elevate you.

The next type of relationship is the protégé. It's very interesting how the protégé needs to serve the leader for a season. I have seen many times how people don't get the anointing of a particular leader because they weren't willing to serve.

My pastor never had to lift a finger for anything. He never had to make any arrangements, because I took care of all of that. It was only because I wanted what he had. I was willing to be his protégé. Some people called me flunky, but I'm the only one who got the message. I knew what I was pursuing.

God looks for servers and promotes them to leadership. You only remember what you are taught. That's why it is so important when we get a revelation to make sure that we find someone to share that revelation with so that we will both remember.

And if ye have not been faithful in that which is another man's, who shall give you that which is your own? **Luke 16:12**

In a protégé relationship you have to be faithful in another man's ministry. If you were ever critical in another person's ministry, then, there will be people around to criticize you. What are you producing? We have to be looking for a protégé.

The fathers have to look for someone who is worthy. Remember, you must stay linked together and finally, in the third type of relationship, you must have friends with those people who will feed your strengths; not your weaknesses.

You want to have friends who pray with you, instead of talk about you. You need friends who will encourage you when you're down, rather than have a pity party with you. You need a friend who will stick closer than a brother.

These relationship concepts of mentor, protégé and friend will Apostolically equip you for the Prophetic to manifest itself in your life.

PROPHETIC POINTS TO REMEMBER

- The Apostle Paul said in Romans 8:6, "to be carnally minded is death." The word *carnal* comes from the root *carne* for meat and *head* represents the *mind*. So, what he is telling us, "Don't be a meat head!"
- The most important relationships are often those that profoundly changed us and made a difference in our lives.

THE STILL SMALL VOICE IN THE GAME OF LIFE

Chapter 7
THE VALUE OF PROPHETIC ANOINTING

It is important to place value on the Prophetic anointing. Certain things have great worth and the way people handle these items is based on their value. For example, a diamond watch. If a person understands the value of that diamond watch they will handle it more carefully.

What I'm going to do with the Word is tell you the worth of the anointing. So, when you hear that someone says that you have a Prophetic anointing on your life, you will see all that comes with it. You'll understand the entire package.

PRINCIPLE 1
Inquire of God

You have the ability to access God. The Prophetic anointing allows you to inquire of God on behalf of other people or for yourself.

PRINCIPLE 2
Settling Differences and Disputes

You have the ability to settle differences and disputes between individuals, businesses, churches, etc. You should remember that each one of us has been Born Again and has the ministry of reconciliation.

The Prophetic anointing helps you in that reconciliation process. Anybody that does any counseling, I guarantee you, praying for the Prophetic anointing was the first thing that you needed to do before you counseled.

The anointing will cut your counseling time down because when you settle differences everyone knows who is wrong. You can see right through the junk and smoke screens people put up.

PRINCIPLE 3
Makes Known God's Statutes and Laws

The Prophetic anointing makes known His statutes and legal system He has instituted for His people.

Furthermore, the Prophetic mantle helps you to accurately interpret the Word of God and communicate it to others in daily living. The prophetic mantle magnifies your ability to take scriptures and apply them to your daily walk.

Sometimes you might have heard a great sermon but there was no revelation given and so, you had no understanding of it. It had no practical application for your life. What the Prophetic mantle will do is take that Word, interpret it, and communicate it so the hearers can walk it out.

PRINCIPLE 4
Provides God's counsel

When you know God's counsel on a matter it is your responsibility to discuss it with God first, then, with those around you. The Prophetic mantle will answer questions concerning those you counsel, those around them and even the nation, as desired by the Lord.

> And when they shall say unto you, Seek unto them that have familiar spirits, and unto wizards that peep, and that mutter: should not a people seek unto their God? For the living to the dead? **Isaiah 8:19**

> To the law and to the testimony: if they speak not according to this word, [it is] because [there is] no light in them.
> **Isaiah 8:20**

In other words, we're living in a day and time when even a lot of Christian people seek out horoscopes, 900 numbers and other sources of mediums and sorcery because there was no Prophetic voice available to them.

If the horoscopes and mediums do not tell them something that is totally contrary to the Word of God, some will act on what they were told. The Prophetic anointing helps us to distinguish who is speaking and gives us understanding of it, as well as information.

Know the source of the information. Who told you? Notice what God told Adam and Eve. God didn't tell them they were not naked because they were. The question He asked them was, "Who told you that you were naked?" Genesis 3:11.

The questions to ask regarding the source of the information is who told you and for what purpose. So you have to understand that there are a variety of sources where we can get information. The ultimate purpose of the other sources is to take you away from God.

PRINCIPLE 5
Guides Us through all Situations

God shows us the way we are to walk through a particular situation. The Prophetic mantle requires certain things of you to walk through it. What is required of me may not be what is required of you.

This comes out of that personal relationship you have with God. You can't allow other people to box you into their way of responding to God. The emphasis must always be on developing a close relationship with God so you can respond to Him in your own special way.

PRINCIPLE 6
Shows Us the Call of God On Our Lives

God's desire is to show us the work He wants us to do, what our assignment is. We should be led by the Spirit of God; not by pain. Most people are led by pain and discomfort and not by the Holy Spirit.

For instance, why do people leave the churches they used to attend? In many cases it's because they got offended. The problem with that is if you left there offended, then, you take that offended seed to the next church and so on.

> Be not deceived; God is not mocked: for whatsoever a man soweth, that shall he also reap. **Galatians 6:7**

This is the principle to live by when joining or leaving a church. Be mindful of the seeds you plant and the ones you to take with you and plant somewhere else. You should never leave a church upset. Instead of staying offended, pray for wisdom and sow seeds of reconciliation and peace.

The same thing happens in relationships. If you broke the last relationship and it didn't heal, then, the next person you have a relationship with pays for the mess the previous person made. That's why you have to get healed. Those of you who have the prophetic mantle have the responsibility to stay connected with God.

PRINCIPLE 7
Deliver Widespread Revelation

Prophetic people have to make declarations to break the heavens so that the heavens open. Those who are prophetic must see and discern what is in the invisible or spiritual realm and pull it to the visible, natural realm.

This is done by praying and speaking Prophetically. We birth it through prayer and speaking so that it manifests. Prophetic people have the ability and the power through the anointing to bring widespread revelation to many.

During Jesus' time, there were two main groups of believers, the Jesus only followers and the John the Baptist only followers. So, Jesus prophetically prayed and declared the revelation of both to become widespread. You are the result of that.

> And the child Samuel ministered unto the LORD before Eli. And the word of the LORD was precious in those days; [there was] no open vision. **1 Samuel 3:1**

THE VALUE OF PROPHETIC ANOINTING

Just like Samuel, you are being trained in the Prophetic individually, in churches and through the electronic media that is making this revelation knowledge widespread. There was no widespread revelation during Samuel's day!

PRINCIPLE 8
Receive Revelation

The prophetic mantle helps you to receive revelation of what God's will is. There are some people who have no idea what the will of God is for their lives or the lives of others. You could have knocked me in the head, but I knew that my daughter was supposed to go to the University of Michigan.

I knew that she was supposed to sing and dance. So all of the training she received was incorporated with the knowledge of her purpose. Only when you know the will of God can you function such a certain way.

Very interesting that if you know the will of God you can also put your treasures toward God's will. If you don't know where the will of God is you'll spread your money everywhere.

> I will be his father, and he shall be my son: and I will not take my mercy away from him, as I took [it] from [him] that was before thee: **1 Chronicles 17:13**

But I will settle him in mine house and in my kingdom for ever: and his throne shall be established for evermore. **1 Chronicles 17:14**

The Prophet Nathan spoke these words and visions to David. With certain individuals as they begin to talk, you can perceive and recognize the will of God for their life.

And, you, as a prophetic person, especially if you're in a family with no revelation or insight, have real opportunity to give direct inside instruction to shine the light in a world of darkness as you start to understand the will of God.

PRINCIPLE 9
Receive Revelation & Communicate the Vision

You have to see yourself as an antenna that has the ability to receive and also the ability to communicate what you receive. You are a receiver and transmitter.

Some people do not have any idea what God is saying because they don't have the ability to catch the signal God is transmitting. Some individuals who receive the signal have trouble articulating it. That's where the Prophetic anointing makes a way for them.

There have been many Prophets who stuttered and stammered in the natural, but under the anointing spoke fluently. There was Moses and also, Oral Roberts.

PRINCIPLE 10
Points People to God through Repentance

One of the purposes of the Prophetic anointing is to take your temperature and that of other individuals to gauge their relationship with God.

Whether they are hot or cold the Prophetic anointing will move them back toward their correct spiritual temperature through repentance. We get the word 'penance' from the same root meaning of repentance, the desire to be forgiven. Penance is the action showing sorrow for a wrong doing.

When you change your mind you will change your behavior. If you change your behavior you create new habits. The prophetic has the ability to move people back into the correct relationship with God.

PRINCIPLE 11
Judge and Discern

The Prophetic anointing judges and discerns individuals and nations. What I mean by this is there are people who will attempt to hide from you because they know you're going to talk to them about God and they do not want to hear it.

That is the dimension I speak of where people know that you can see through them. They don't want to do right things so they hide from you.

PRINCIPLE 12
Prophesy Positions on Contemporary Matters

There are certain contemporary matters that you and I can tap into to see how God feels about that particular issue.

The Prophetic anointing will give you access to God and knowledge about how He feels regarding a contemporary issue. This special access is based on your relationship with Him.

PRINCIPLE 13
Reveals the Thoughts of a Man's Heart

Revealing the thoughts of a man speaks to the capacity for reading a man's heart. There are times when the prophetic has the ability to read the thoughts of your own heart to know exactly what your motives are.

One of the reasons why I am so involved in this whole thing is because when I got saved the Pastor read my heart. Prior to that, the only one I knew who was talking to me was the devil. God wasn't speaking to me and He wasn't speaking to anyone else I knew.

Yet, the devil was talking to me *all* the time. So when I went to this particular church the preacher got up and said that someone here sees certain things, perceives things. Well, I just thought that everybody was having the same experiences as I was having.

For the first time in my life I could identify with somebody who knew what I was feeling, thinking and seeing. My life was transformed through the Prophetic word. Preaching didn't transform my life. I heard people preach before. It was the prophetic word I received that caused me to want to study God's Word.

> And Samuel answered Saul, and said, I [am] the seer: go up before me unto the high place; for ye shall eat with me to day, and to morrow I will let thee go, and will tell thee all that [is] in thine heart. **1 Samuel 9:19**

PRINCIPLE 14
Anoint and Integrate Leaders for Service

This reflects the spiritual and natural authority of a prophet to install and empower those who will be leaders in God's kingdom. The Prophetic anointing is what anoints people for position.

In the Old Testament prophets anointed kings, they anointed priests, and prophets anointed other prophets. The prophetic has the ability to activate, stir up and pull out the King, the priest, the prophet, the leader and/or the assignment that is inside of you.

PRINCIPLE 15
Counsel and Enlighten Leaders

If you are not in full time ministry but have a Prophetic anointing on you, you can enlighten your leader by remaining humble and just open and share what God gives you.

God gives us a Word, and if we are to share it, then, we share it and take on the responsibility not to force someone to do it. You never want to manipulate or control anything.

For example, you tell somebody that they're not supposed to go to a school and, then, they go anyway. Don't take control and try to make them do what you've prophetically told them to do because that is the wrong spirit.

I just simply share the Word, share what God has given me. In this respect, I become the mailman. I bring good mail or bad mail, I'm just the messenger, but don't kill the messenger if you don't like the message!

PRINCIPLE 16
Inspire Spiritual Perception

There are people, and you'll see with the Prophetic anointing, whose hearts are hard and they are cold. The prophetic has the ability to penetrate that.

I love coldhearted people. I minister to people who are coldhearted, mad at God, and mad at the world. Once you get them in front of you that revelation of God will begin to calm them. As the anointing begins to increase, it will begin to break the cold-heartedness. It's similar to a salvation experience.

Have you seen someone get Born Again? Their face lights up and they cry for joy? Well, an accurate Prophetic Word does the same thing; it pierces through to the heart of the matter.

> [Is it] not wheat harvest to day? I will call unto the LORD, and he shall send thunder and rain; that ye may perceive and see that your wickedness [is] great, which ye have done in the sight of the LORD, in asking you a king. **1 Samuel 12:17**

The Prophet's job, in the above scripture, was to help the people perceive how God felt about that particular situation.

Now that you know your value and worth in the prophetic I challenge you to step into it!

PROPHETIC PRINCIPLES TO REMEMBER

- The Prophetic Anointing gives us the ability to Inquire of God.
- The Prophetic Anointing gives us the ability to Settle Differences and Disputes.
- The Prophetic Anointing makes known God's Statutes and Laws.
- The Prophetic Anointing Provides God's counsel.
- The Prophetic Anointing guides us through all situations.
- The Prophetic Anointing shows us the Call of God on our lives.
- The Prophetic Anointing delivers widespread Revelation.
- The Prophetic Anointing gives us the ability to receive Revelation.
- The Prophetic Anointing gives us the ability to receive revelation and communicate God's vision.
- The Prophetic Anointing points people to God through repentance.
- The Prophetic Anointing judges and discerns.
- The Prophetic Anointing gives us the ability to prophesy positions on contemporary matters.
- The Prophetic Anointing reveals the thoughts of a man's heart.
- The Prophetic Anointing Anoints and Integrates Leaders for Service.
- The Prophetic Anointing counsels and enlightens leaders.
- The Prophetic Anointing inspires spiritual perception.

Chapter 8
PRINCIPLES OF THE PROPHETIC

The Principles that I share will cause your Prophetic gift to be sharpened. Your gift will be sharper, and sharper because of the things of God that I am about to walk you through. You are about to go from a vague and generic kind of understanding to a very specific one.

Regardless of what level you are at, by the time it's all over you will be able to move up to the next level. Principles work whether you know them or not. Principles are working for you or against you. The more principles you understand, the more successful you will tend to be.

I don't care who you are or what your status is, how smart or uninformed you are, it doesn't matter. It's as sure as the Law of

Gravity works, whether you understand it or not. What goes up must come down.

Even an airplane does not violate the law of gravity. It only temporarily supersedes it through the Law of Lift. Likewise, the prophetic is irrepressible and if you understand these principles you will become stronger and be lifted higher.

I've watched some people and have observed that they didn't become stronger and seemed to stay at the same level. They stayed at the same level because they did not understand the principles. They stumbled, bobbled and fumbled upon hearing the voice of God. For them, it wasn't an active, everyday part of their life.

As you adjust your mindset, as you adjust your schedule, and adjust yourself to some of the principles, you will experience a greater degree of success. The goal is to make you comfortable so that when you prophesy you speak God's perfect will.

PRINCIPLE 1
Desire to Prophesy

You must desire to prophesy. You must have a white hot passionate desire for prophecy. Otherwise, you'll have the 'I only deserve to receive crumbs that fall from the Master's table' mentality. That won't do.

God wants to minister to you. He wants to talk to you. Have you ever tried to talk to someone who didn't want to talk to you? No matter how bad you wanted to talk to them they still didn't want to talk to you.

> Follow after charity, and desire spiritual [gifts], but rather that ye may prophesy. **1 Corinthians 14:1**

> For he that speaketh in an [unknown] tongue speaketh not unto men, but unto God: for no man understandeth [him]; howbeit in the spirit he speaketh mysteries. **1 Corinthians 14:2**

> But he that prophesieth speaketh unto men [to] edification, and exhortation, and comfort. **1 Corinthians 14:3 1 Corinthians 14:2**

The above passage of scripture shows us why we need to focus in on the prophetic. This is why some people get confused and others label certain things as being prophetic. It becomes limited in its scope. You can get comfortable in that manifestation.

In the course of this book, we are going to do some things that are specifically geared toward prophetic knowledge that has a broad scope to it. Come with me, let's expand our understanding!

PRINCIPLE 2
Prove every Word

Prove every word that comes out of your mouth. A lot of times we are allowed to practice everything but the prophetic. Has anyone ever been to a church when someone was singing and the singing was bad but they let them sing anyway?

Those bad singers were allowed to practice. Yet, when it comes to the prophetic we want people to suddenly be mature in their gift. Prophets of old had schools where they spent time in the company of other prophets and were seasoned. They had a place where their gift could be practiced and perfected.

Even when Samuel first heard the voice of God, he was hearing it in the prophetic. Elijah had enough information to recognize the voice of God. When you get a Word you have to able to prove that Word. None of us get so great that our Word cannot be proven.

I tell people what the Lord says, and I give them a tape recording so they can take it back to their pastor(s) to be judged. That word will stand the test of time. We want to be proved because if it is God, it will stand.

Normally, when you have a flaky prophet and you pull out a tape recorder they will get scared. And there might be times when you are in the spirit you miss things. A lot of times we miss things.

When you get home you can sit and listen to the Word you gave. You will hear something you missed the first time. That's why we enjoy watching the same movies over and over again. We get something different and fresh out of them each time.

The best candidates for the prophetic are those who have a solid foundation of the Word of God and in prophetic principles, and who are willing to allow their words to be judged.

Once you reach a certain status there is a temptation to become afraid to say the words God is giving them because they don't want to miss the prophetic mark. It might be that their reputation is too important to them. But when you don't have a reputation you can step all the way out in faith!

The proving process will help you get stronger and stronger even though there might still be a time or two when you miss something. It's comparable to a professional basketball player who is paid millions of dollars, and still misses some shots.

In the prophetic, we are always trying our best to prophesy accurately, and correctly present what God is saying, but we're still clay vessels.

PRINCIPLE 3
Responsibility

The spirit of the prophet is subject to the prophet, 1 Corinthian 14:32.

Let me repeat, 'The spirit of the Prophet is subject to whom? The prophet, that's who!' Your own spirit is subject to you. You can stir the gift of God up in you or you can squelch it and turn it off. It's up to you.

The following scriptures give the account of the Prophet Elisha and the Shunemite woman. She and her husband were wealthy and blessed Elisha so much that he had to say, 'Wait a minute, what can I do for you?' He asked her if she wanted him to introduce her to the King, but she said 'no.'

Elisha saw that she had money and wealth and didn't need anything. Then, it came to him. She wanted a child because in that culture and custom to be without a child was viewed unfavorably. She was considered an incomplete woman without a child.

The stirred up the prophetic Gift because that woman had blessed him, and he wanted to be a blessing to her. Remember, the spirit of the prophet is subject to the prophet. You can stir up the Gift of God or you can turn it off.

Then, Elisha prophesied to her that she would have a baby by that time the following year, and she did even though her husband was old. Elisha, the Prophet, stirred up the gift within him to bless someone else.

> One day Elisha went to the town of Shunem. A wealthy woman lived there, and she invited him to eat some food. From then on, whenever he passed that way, he would stop there to eat. **2 Kings 4:8**

She said to her husband, "I am sure this man who stops in from time to time is a holy man of God. **2 Kings 4:9**

Let's make a little room for him on the roof and furnish it with a bed, a table, a chair, and a lamp. Then he will have a place to stay whenever he comes by." **2 Kings 4:10**

And it fell on a day, that he came thither, and he turned into the chamber, and lay there. **2 Kings 4:11**

He said to his servant Gehazi, "Tell the woman I want to speak to her." When she arrived, **2 Kings 4:12**

Elisha said to Gehazi, "Tell her that we appreciate the kind concern she has shown us. Now ask her what we can do for her. Does she want me to put in a good word for her to the king or to the commander of the army?" "No," she replied, "my family takes good care of me." **2 Kings 4:13**

Later Elisha asked Gehazi, "What do you think we can do for her?" He suggested, "She doesn't have a son, and her husband is an old man." **2 Kings 4:14**

"Call her back again," Elisha told him. When the woman returned, Elisha said to her as she stood in the doorway, **2 Kings 4:15**

"Next year at about this time you will be holding a son in your arms!" "No, my lord!" she protested. "Please don't lie to me like that, O man of God." **2 Kings 4:16**

But sure enough, the woman soon became pregnant. And at that time the following year she had a son, just as Elisha had said. **2 Kings 4:17** *New Living Translation*

There are some people that when they come around, I turn off the Gift. Early in my prophetic walk I wanted to say everything. And, I was really nosy. I wanted to know everyone's business. But now I don't because I've learned how to turn it on and off.

Learning how to turn it off is very important because it teaches you how to control your spirit. God has made us free will agents and we have to learn how to control our own spirit.

But without faith [it is] impossible to please [him]: for he that cometh to God must believe that he is, and [that] he is a rewarder of them that diligently seek him. **Hebrews 11:6**

You've got to work with God and exercise your faith because He wants to get you to your destiny. You have to work with God in order for your prophetic to come to pass. It's His desire that you work with His plan for your life. We are laborers together with Him. We have to learn how to respond to the spirit of God.

There are times when we'll have an unction to prophesy. Yet, other times, we don't have an unction to flow in the gifts. The definition of unction is "a fervent passion to anoint." That says it all!

God wants us, also, to have joy in this. We have to learn how to enjoy the spiritual moves of God. If your spirit is not fun to you, then, it won't be fun to anyone else. If you are not sure in your salvation, then, no one else will want to be saved.

If you don't enjoy your church, then, no one will want to go to your church when you invite them. Why would they? How many people would say to you that they want to go to your church after you have talked negatively about it?

The same thing applies with worship. If you don't enjoy worshipping God, why would a sinner want what you have? You have to be excited in order or someone else to be excited. Remember, if it is not blessing you, it is not going to bless me.

PRINCIPLE 4
Accountability

You have to be accountable for the Word you share. You have to be willing to say that you missed it when you miss it. Own up to it. None of us ever want to be wrong. But that's part of the whole process that we go through.

You are responsible to make sure that you cultivate the gift to maturity. When God gives you a gift it is your responsibility to make sure that gift increases. If you give him the gift the same way he gave it to you, then, he calls you an unprofitable servant.

So my responsibility, as I discover which gift of the spirit I am given, is to nurture it. If I'm called to five fold ministry, it is my obligation to develop that calling. That's my job!

Don't forget to be accountable and sensitive to your pastor and the leadership of your church. I cannot take the church in a direction that I want it to go. It has to be the Lord's direction. Is it ok for me to touch on this subject? Very rarely does God direct you to tear up the place.

I will never forget when I was in Memphis, on TBN one time. There was a guy who was very offensive. I offended him and he offended me. I was young, then, and didn't know any better. The service was supposed to begin at 11:00am and instead it began at 11:45am, forty five minutes after the time the service was supposed to start. So, I said I think we ought to begin.

I was going to start another man's service which was out of order. I started his service and started singing, and about 12:00 it was time to prophesy. But I was in somebody else's house taking control of it and that was totally wrong.

The pastor came back out to the podium, and he talked about me for a half hour. He started preaching, and as he was preaching he jumped right on me. As this was going on, the Lord started showing me errors in this man's church. And I thought to myself, 'I'm going to tear this place up!'

Everything that the man had done wrong, I knew it. I could see it precisely, dates, times, situations. Paul said, "I use my knowledge for edification and not destruction." So I sat down and cried, because I had information about him that God was telling me not to use.

Why wouldn't God let me use the information He showed me about this man and his church? Because it was a test to see how I would handle it, and I failed the test by being out of order. I reacted to the offense I felt by trying to take control of the service.

Even though I had information that could have helped that pastor, he wouldn't have received it, because I had been acting out of the wrong spirit. These issues were going on in my head. So, I didn't tear the place up. I felt like God was killing me with what He was showing me. He wanted to see how I would handle it.

You have to come to the place, that, when you have certain information about someone or a situation that you are not destructive with it, or out of order.

PRINCIPLE 5
Prophetic Layering

This is when several people prophesy over an individual. One of the things is that you don't want to prophesy too long over that person. Why? Because if you have to prophesy over a group of people and you prophesy over one person too long, what happens? The faith level of everyone else drops.

People will calculate that if you spent 20 minutes prophesying to just one person that you'd never get to them! And so the whole level of faith drops. If you give a short prophecy over each person, then, the others will think that their chances of you prophesying over them are good and therefore, the faith level remains high.

More than that, certain individuals don't have much faith that what you are saying is from God if the prophesy is too long. But the truth of the matter is, when you're standing on the flood gates of prophecy, as long as you are there the flood waters keep coming down.

Even so, in the mindset of certain individuals, God only says a few words. So, remember not to go beyond your measure of rule. If God says only prophesy to the women, then, that's what you will only do. If God says only minister to the couples, then, that's all you do. There is a measure of authority you have that you can not violate.

PRINCIPLE 6
Faith

Faith activates the prophetic. If you do not believe that the prophetic is for you, then, the prophetic will not work in your life. If you don't have faith, then, by this Dispensation, the prophetic will not operate because your faith is working against you, instead of for you.

That's why, in some cases, we have to bring information before revelation. Gifts differ but they all must be exercised in order to increase your faith. And, sometimes there has to be a manifestation of God's presence for the people of God to believe that God is in that place.

Your attitude should be that you always want to use your Gift. When I started out and didn't have anywhere to use my gift, I went to the mall and used it there. I looked for any opportunity to use it.

You should do the same thing. Look for a place where you can minister prophetically. The more you use your gifting, the more developed it becomes. In order to increase your faith, you must *exercise* your faith.

PRINCIPLE 7
Spirit of Liberty

We must keep our conscience clear. Don't let anything stop you. What the enemy will do is attempt to hinder you.

> For if I make you sorry, who is he then that maketh me glad, but the same which is made sorry by me? **2 Corinthians 2:2**

> For out of much affliction and anguish of heart I wrote unto you with many tears; not that ye should be grieved, but that ye might know the love which I have more abundantly unto you. **2 Corinthians 2:4**

My responsibility is to keep myself in position so that I can minister. That's why if I'm somewhere and someone makes me angry, I get out of there. Why? Because my gift stops up if I'm mad at you.

If something bad happens I try to clear it up as soon as possible because I can become ineffective in ministering if I stay in a bad frame of mind. God cannot use me if I'm upset, and I don't want to give anyone that kind of power over my life, except God.

PRINCIPLE 8
Timing

In other words, when should you prophesy and for how long? I have watched people prophesy at the wrong time which changed the course of the service.

The preacher is up front and people were in a corner prophesying! It was out of order. God is a God of order.

For example, if you're sitting on the platform and need to go to the bathroom don't just get up and leave. Operating in order would be to stand up, excuse yourself, and then walk to the restroom. When it comes to prophecy we must learn how to restrain our Gifting.

I've been in places where I wish I could have been doing the preaching. There are two times when a preacher really wants to preach and that is when the message is real good and the message is real bad! But when you have a clear urging from the Spirit of God you'll flow according to the order of the house of God.

The final principle is the usage of wisdom and as a side note, there are public words and private words. There are some words you say to certain individuals only in private.

One of the mistakes that prophetically led people make is that they give private words in public. Although the Word may be accurate it is ineffective and out of order because the word was meant to be in private.

Always consult God when you do not know what to say. Remember the beginning of wisdom is the fear of the Lord according to Psalm 111:10.

PROPHETIC PRINCIPLES TO REMEMBER

- You must Desire to Prophesy.
- You must Prove Every Word that comes out of your mouth.
- You have Responsibility for own spirit.
- You must have Accountability for the Word you share.
- Limit the length of your prophecy when there are other prophets prophesying to the same individual.
- Faith activates the prophetic.
- There must be Liberty to prophesy, a clear conscience free of guilt, strife or sin.
- Timing; knowing when to prophesy and how long to prophesy.

Chapter 9
SUN STANDS STILL

Your uniqueness and relationship with God determines your greatness. During certain seasons you need certain people. There are certain seasons in your life. You need certain individuals in your life in a season of war.

When you are in a season of war, you must make sure you have warriors with you. You must have intercessory warriors with you. I need a group of people who know how to target an issue and stay there until they get a breakthrough.

When I headed to spiritual battle or war, I didn't ask everyone with me. I took certain people with me, who knew how to fight. It was not time to train people. I was only 25 years old. The reason why I stayed married was because my wife knew that I had a "fight" in me.

It seemed like I always had a battle on the horizon. But when you know that you're going to war you become aware that you are ready to birth something. You need certain people with you. When it's for celebration, you need a certain group of people who know how to celebrate.

When you are in times of war it's because you are getting ready to possess the land, disinherit something, and dispossess somebody from your house. You need to have a certain type of individual with a certain mentality. I believe God is raising individuals with like mindedness to walk alongside with you.
You disconnect with some individuals and reconnect with others because when you are angry you want to possess the things of God. We have a warrior mentality. There was no one around me to calm it down. I needed someone around me to edge me on.

Joshua was able to get individuals who were ready for war. So here is Joshua and he had some people with him that were ready for war. He had some people who were proven in battle and were not going to give up.

You need somebody that will fight and pray without ceasing, not going to stop or give up the cause. When we mobilize ourselves there is going to be an opportunity for you to fear. As soon as this happens there are going to be some ugly folks coming your way.

There are going to be some bullies and their goal is to intimidate you. They come into your life to keep you from doing what God wants you to do.

For example, you might tell your girlfriends that you want a man, and they are there to discourage you. They will say you can never get the man of your dreams, so you might as well as eat that cake and add the extra pounds!

A life with God and those bullies is not God's plan for you. In relationships there are some people who are there to destroy you. This is a classic example of God working with you in accomplishing His will in the earth.

There are some things that you can do in this life, but there are some things that only God can do. Christians often get the wrong mindset by expecting God to do everything. I would not bless you if you're not paying your tithes and neither will God.

People are usually not blessed because they will not obey God's command. One of the things about all this is that I believe God desires to restore the elements working with us, instead of the elements working *for* us.

I know it sounds a little crazy but I think what happens is we have to give the information first, then, the revelation comes forth. There cannot be revelation without information. So someone has to come along with crazy ideas and begin to preach about it, then, God will anoint and take the veil off it. Once the veil is removed you're able to see it. Then, you can act on it. I believe here we see a classic example of how God became involved in the affairs of men. I believe that God in the book of Genesis established Adam. He gave Adam dominion and authority over everything.

Adam sinned and lost his measure of that authority. Through Jesus that authority was restored. But what often happens is that a lot of us are afraid to step out on faith. We feel it's abnormal so we wouldn't dare try to do some of those things because we don't know anyone else who's doing those things.

I have been having Conferences for over 10 years in a cold climate. During that same period of time, not one Conference has been snowed out because of the fact that we believe we can speak to the snow and tell it, back up!

When we started to talk about having the Conference everyone said, 'You're crazy! Ya'll are going to get snowed out!' No, we weren't crazy, and we weren't going to get snowed out. We knew then, and now, that we have authority over the elements.

If we are doing it in the time frame God has ordained, then, we can speak to the elements and the elements must obey because of the authority we have over those things.

I will never forget at one of our church's first picnics I was working for the youth at the time. The old time holiness members didn't believe in picnics and didn't believe in sports, period! No basketball, volleyball, or softball. They thought is all was a SIN.

The only thing they believed in was going to church. And that's why we were a church only consisting of old folks. They did not have opportunities for the youth. The young people thought the church was boring and dead. So I decided that I was going to take the youth to the park for a picnic.

Once there, it started thundering and lightning and all the old folks said that it was the devil! That if it was the Lord, the Lord would not have it thundering and lightning.

There I was, young and stupid, polluted into believing what the old folks were saying. It was raining, it wasn't God's will for us to be at the park, and believing that I started loading up the van. I loaded food, charcoal, everything while it was lightning.

But then, I said, "Lord, if you don't stop this thunder and lightning I will not serve you. I will go back into the world because you don't love these kids." Well, God knows our heart. He knows how we are. He knows that we don't always say the right things. He knows that sometimes we don't know what we are talking about.

Even so, God began to move because of His plan to let those children fellowship with godly people, and reveal to them that He wants us to have fun.

The rain backed up so much that we barbecued. We had a great time because God was concerned with the future that He had in store for those children. And from that time on I had everyone in our church involved with recreational, as well as spiritual, activities.

The elements are subject to you. We were in Memphis, Tennessee and having a tent revival. I had an entire itinerary of activities planned for outdoors because the elements are subject to us. We were there when the forecast called for rain 10 days straight.

I told everyone that the rain would stop when I got there. It did, in fact, stop raining. Every activity that we had planned for outdoors we were able to have because we commanded the weather not to interfere with what we were doing.

The night that Jesus was betrayed He was praying. He knew that God had promised to be with Him as He was with Moses. When Jesus was praying to the Father, He said, 'I know you always hear me, but I am praying this in the midst of these individuals, so they will know that You hear when I prophesy.' He didn't want God to tell Him after the event.

Don't tell me after the event. Don't tell me, after everything is over. Tell me before the thing happens. So you, Lord, have a witness. Also, so I can believe in your gifting. However, if you tell me something after the fact, I don't believe you, and the devil is going to tell me not to believe you, and I will listen to him.

So you have to know that prophecies are designed to come in advance. Tell me something in advance. Have you ever seen someone come to a church and it does not work out for them? They'll say, 'I could have told you first because the Lord showed me.'

I say to those people, 'Why didn't you tell me a long time ago?' Don't tell me after I have hit my head against the wall and made bad decisions. If the Lord first showed you, then, so tell me.

Do you realize that the average ministry has about a five year success rate? Then, you go back into the woodwork. You become ordinary again. You have to know when your time is. What is your cutting edge time? When is it your growth spurt?

You have to ride the wave and work with God while He's doing that. If your season is over, you just blend back into the background. So it is important to be like the sons of Isschar who understood the time of God and the seasons of God.

When it's your time and your season, you can speak to the sun and it has to obey you. Speak to your circumstances and they have to obey you, because it's my time. But, now the problem is that sometimes we don't know when our time is.

You have to understand, what is your season? You can become pregnant at any time but you can't deliver the baby until it is time. You can't just jump up and say that I am going to have a baby tonight. There is a season and a time for everything to gather for that purpose. It's the same way with God.

There is a season in time when God is doing certain things. You've got to work with Him, and let Him guide you in order for the fullness to be in your life. Testimony is what God used to do or what He has done, past tense.

If you know what God is doing in your life, then, you will always be on the cutting edge. You will constantly be on a current wave and continually have something fresh.

Just like Saul, I listen to singers by listening to worship music. There are certain songs that the keyboard player plays that produces the anointing of God because God is anointing that song for that time and season. And so the "worshippers" responsibility is to play before God and listen for that sound so that the anointing of God will come.

It's the same with a preacher. A preacher has to stay before God in order for God's Spirit, His anointing, to be there. Now, He spoke to the Son and said, "Son, I want you to stay where You are." In order for me to complete destiny, in order for me to kill my enemies today, I need you to stand still right now.

In the mean time, you're feeling like you can't wait another day. I have to get this person tonight. Glory to God! I can't wait anymore. If I don't get it now, I'm not going to get it at all. There has to be sense of urgency with your destiny.

I can't wait until next year, I can't wait until the next move of God, I have to get it right now. I want to be in the place where God is currently moving. I'm lying out before God and everything else has to stand still. I have to speak to God in those situations.

It becomes subject to the man or woman of God who understands who they are and what power they possess. If I tell my son to sit there and not move, I expect him to sit there and not move. Why? Because he understands my authority. He has been trained. That's the expectation that I have for him as his father.

I expect him to behave because of the authority that is in his life. Through your obedience, God wants you to defeat the devil. He wants the devil to be defeated in your life because every time you defeat the devil God gets the glory.

The devil was in Heaven and he believed that he could control Heaven. The devil was playing the keyboard and saying that God was not that smart. He believed that his music was so beautiful that it would beguile everyone. He believed that he could do a better job than God, but God just turned to the devil and threw him and his boys out of Heaven.

In so many words, God said, 'Get your butt out of my house!' Now, He threw them down to the earth and God told the angels that He was going to take the dirt and breathe life into it. More than that, God was going to give this dirt authority over the devil. Every time this dirt defeats the devil it shows how awesome I Am that I Am is.

He's still telling the devil that he can not even beat the dust that He made. Glory to God! That's why He says that you will always be triumphant. You stand still for God to realize or recognize what the Father is saying. When we begin to follow what Daddy says we'll always come out victorious!

One thing that you want to recognize is that you have been fearfully and wonderfully made. God has made you unique. Some people don't understand the beauty of their uniqueness. We shy away from being special because we try to look like others, dress like them, act like them, and be just like them.

When you do that you lose your unique individuality. 1 Samuel 17:38-39 speaks to this issue.

> And Saul armed David with his armour, and he put an helmet of brass upon his head; also he armed him with a coat of mail. **1 Samuel 17:38**

> And David girded his sword upon his armour, and he assayed to go; for he had not proved [it]. And David said unto Saul, I cannot go with these; for I have not proved [them]. And David put them off him. **1 Samuel 17:39**

Israel is fighting against the Philistines and they are equally matched. The victory was in the knowledge of how to use the armor. David hadn't learned to use it in battle.

Ask yourself, what do you need to be successful in battle? There needs to be a transformation in order for you to be successful. David put on Saul's armor but it was too big and didn't fit him, because he was just a teenager.

So, David said, 'Listen, I have to pull this off because I can't fight effectively with it. I can't do what God is calling me to do, that is, kill Goliath, in another man's armor. If I do, Goliath will kill me!'

A lot of times we are destroyed because we are trying to do it the way other folks have done it. This is the way that it has always been done. For example, some churches have great success with bus ministries, but we didn't. Yet we tried.

We bought our first bus around 1983. It was a big old yellow bus. We got that big old yellow bus and took it down to the station. We said we're going to use it to win souls for the Lord. That ugly bus could not even pass the vehicle inspection.

The guy who sold it to me said that, "That's why I gave you that bus for a cheap price because I knew it couldn't pass the inspection."

I tried the bus ministry and we lost money on it. I never could convince anyone, not even children, to ride that bus. We used to drive into the housing projects hoping to win souls. But we considered ourselves blessed not to get stoned for pulling that monster of a bus in there!

Our prayer became not for souls but for the bus not to break down while trying to get people to the House of the Lord. The bus ministry did not work for us; it was not our purpose. It didn't work because we were copying somebody else's ministry. Tell yourself that you need to stop copying off other people.

Have you ever been in school and you copied off someone's paper and got the wrong answer just like they did? If I'm going to fail I'm going to fail by myself. There may be a wrong thing in your life like Saul's armor on David.

Saul wanted David to dress like him, he wanted him to think like him, he wanted him to fight like him, but David's victory was in his own, special, distinct, unique relationship with God. David's uniqueness. Uniqueness! The plan is always giving out of your relationship with God, not someone else's.

For every man there is a special plan. Your job is to spend time in your relationship with God, and out of that relationship He will help you understand what that plan is and why you are the way you are.

There's a lady at my church who fights everything that she sees. She's abrasive. I said to God, "God, why is she so abrasive?" And God said it was because she's an intercessor and designed to have an ongoing war with the devil. She loves to fight. Now, if you don't understand that about yourself, you will fight saints who are fighting the devil.

Put that fighting woman in a spiritual battle and she will come out on top every time because she is a fighter. It's the way she is wired. And so your uniqueness will cause your greatness to come out. This only occurs when you learn and understand why you are wired the way you are.

In Exodus 33:11 we see that God is describing his relationship with Moses. It was a unique relationship just as yours is.

> And the LORD spake unto Moses face to face, as a man speaketh unto his friend. And he turned again into the camp: but his servant Joshua, the son of Nun, a young man, departed not out of the tabernacle.
> **Exodus 33:11**

The Lord spoke unto Moses as a man speaks to his friend, face to face. So, we see here there has never been a man like this who had a face to face encounter with God and talked to him as a friend.

In our New Covenant we have all been elevated to friendship status with Christ Jesus because of what Christ Jesus did on the cross of Calvary. Every one of us has been elevated into friendship status.

But Moses' relationship with God was before the New Covenant, so it was a unique relationship. We can also cultivate a unique relationship with God. You are doing things for God because you are His friend. Write this down, there are certain things that happen out of friendship that will not occur out of law that you cannot legislate.

PROPHETIC POINT

Throughout history, mountains have been scaled, music written, cures for diseases discovered, monuments built and races won because of friendship.

I don't do things out of obligation for my friends because I'm required to do it. I do it because it's the right thing to do for my friend. I'll do things out of a solid relationship that I won't do for any other reason.

I will go places, I will bend over backwards for people that I am in a relationship with that I won't do for other individuals. Now certain friends you will open up your heart and share certain secrets with that you haven't told anyone else about.

God says to Moses that their relationship is so unique that He considers Moses His friend and is going to talk to him, plainly, not in parables. He said that He wasn't going to talk to Moses through anyone. He came to talk to him face to face. I believe that God desires everyone to develop a really unique relationship with Him.

And He wants to manifest Himself to you in a unique way, but we have to get outside the box. We have to be able to spread ourselves and raise up our antennas. We must be receptive until God manifests Himself. So why aren't angels manifesting themselves? Is it because we're not ready for that?

Get ready! Get ready! Get ready! Get ready! You've got to open yourself until God manifests Himself in an unusual way. I'll never forget when God said to me that He wanted to see me face to face. I said, "God, I want to interact with you in a way that I have never interacted with You before." And he inspired me to fast and pray.

As I begin to fast and pray I started to feel the presence of the Lord coming through the front door. I started trying to get up and literally see God because I wanted to see Him. But I felt like I was being pressed to the floor and that's what I said, "God I don't think I want to see you. Send me a letter!" Glory to God!

I like God talking in my spirit. He doesn't have to show Himself to me. But I was willing to pay the price for that relationship. How many of you know that when you decide to take someone home forever that there is a cost for that person?

The key word in getting to the point where God will manifest and reveal Himself is, time. Ask yourself, do you want a special relationship with God, or not? My job is to inspire you to long for God so much that He will manifest Himself in your life in such a way that you'll know without a shadow of a doubt that God loves you.

One of the things that we do in the prophetic is speak a word in different languages that only the prophet can understand. Sometimes we get a prophetic word and it is the same word that God's been talking to you about in the closet. It's Him confirming what He says about you.

And, it's all because He loves you.

REMEMBER THESE FOUR POINTS:
PROPHETIC POINT

1) Your uniqueness determines the quality of your friendships.
2) Your uniqueness determines your calling.
3) Your uniqueness determines your level of anointing.
4) Your unique anointing determines your results.

Should God give you a great anointing to just sit around with? The greater the calling, the greater the anointing will be on an individual's life.

The Bible says that it's the anointing that destroys the yoke. David said "anoint me when in the presence of my enemies." If you don't have any enemies, you don't need any anointing. The devil isn't fighting against your mind, or against your pocketbook.

If you're not fighting the devil you aren't going to have any impact. It's only those who have an impact against the kingdom of darkness who God will put an anointing on. He'll put a heavy anointing on them so they can destroy the works of darkness.

If you are not going to go, then I'll go into the world of darkness that they might see the light of our Father in Heaven. It's only when you are going to go into the Kingdom of darkness, around crack addicts, murderers, robbers and rapists, to advance the kingdom of God that you will need a heavy anointing.

The Bible says the kingdom of heaven suffers violence and the violent forcefully advance in the Kingdom of God. In the holiday season, you need to go to a party and say, 'God is here to shine His light upon you!' Start praying in tongues and seize the atmosphere you're in.

I used to love going to Miami's airport. You go to Miami with all those languages down there. I walk through Miami's airport and pray in tongues. That's the most anointed airport I've ever been in. I seize the atmosphere whenever God wants to use me to advance the kingdom.

PROPHETIC POINT
What are you doing to advance the Kingdom of God?

Think of it when you're talking about taking over. You need areas where you can take over. There are some places in Pontiac, Michigan, that I'm going to take over. I have already set my mind, I'm taking over. I want that area. I'm going to advance the Kingdom of God.

I'm not going to put up with the foolishness of the devil in this city. I'm going to advance, move forward. The concept is that of a rubber band. The rubber band will take the ground where it's directed and released to go. And the rubber band is flexible.

God says, "If you aren't advancing the Kingdom of God, the devil will pull you back." The devil wants to intimidate you. So, God is looking for some individuals who are not reactive, but are proactive just like the rubber band.

What can I do to get on the devil's nerves, to cause him to be intimidated by *me*? What I do to advance the name of God? What can I do to establish His name in my job arena? These are questions you should ask yourself.

Instead of you looking to retire from your job, God is trying to get into your place of business to make a difference in the lives of people who will not go to church. Look at things from God's perspective!

A lot of saints are trying to retire, so that they can be at the church full time. While God is trying to get into the work place full time. He's looking for someone who will go and work for Jesus. Slip in there undercover and take over the plant! Get some Bible studies going.

If you are gifted and anointed in a particular area you will see the result of God's anointing on your life. Luke 6:44 says, "For every tree is known by its own fruit. It produces the life that comes from it. The fruit that you bear is an indication of the type of tree you are."

Your anointing will produce results, or the fruit in your life. If you are an evangelist, people should be getting saved.
Wherever they go, whether in the mall, or at the police station, evangelists consistently want to tell them what Jesus is like.

If no one is getting saved, then, you aren't an evangelist. I haven't seen an evangelist, yet, unable to evangelize. It's inside of them and you can see that souls are getting saved as a result of their anointing.

If you tell me that you have a youth ministry, kids should be following you around like Peter Pan. If you are anointed as a youth pastor, preacher or teacher, then, that anointing should produce the fruit of it in your life.

> Again he said unto me, Prophesy upon these **bones**, and say unto them, O ye **dry bones**, hear the word of the LORD. **Ezekiel 37:4**

God told Ezekiel to prophesy to these bones and speak to those dry ones. When I hear a clear word of God my uniqueness is what allows me to immediately do what God says, while other folks have to think about it first.

You learn God's love language through your relationship with Him. How does God deal with you? How do you know it's God?

Ezekiel prophesied to those dry bones, and called them not as they were, but as what they were going to be. He told those bones to live so they might know that God was the Lord. Our responsibility is to speak out what God has declared in every situation.

Thus saith the Lord GOD unto these bones; Behold, I will cause breath to enter into you, and ye shall live: **Ezekiel 37:5**

And I will lay sinews upon you, and will bring up flesh upon you, and cover you with skin, and put breath in you, and ye shall live; and ye shall know that I [am] the LORD. **Ezekiel 37:6**

And I shall put my spirit in you, and ye shall live, and I shall place you in your own land: then shall ye know that I the LORD have spoken [it], and performed [it], saith the LORD. **Ezekiel 37:14**

God says that He will put His spirit in us and we shall live and know that He is the Lord.

See yourself connected with God. Because you are connected with God His life flows through you. Your job is to stay connected with this power at its very source.

Notice here in the above scripture text, the man of God has the boldness to speak to anything, even skeletons. One of the things you will begin to see when you develop and cultivate the Prophetic gift is God will boldly test you. You'll have to get used to talking to people you don't want to talk to.

God will have you speak to situations. In order for God to deal with earthly situations He needs to have someone who is willing to deal with earthly situations; someone to be used as a vessel. But before that happens, He has to have somebody who can see the enemy, and proclaim that the victory is already the Lord's.

Boldness to talk to anyone and boldness to prophesy is talking to *anyone,* about *anything.* One thing we do in our ministry is the pratice of Activation. That is giving someone a Word from the Lord you do not know.

So when you begin to minister it will be an accurate time to work, and you will have the boldness to say it.

Glory to God! Forever and Ever!

PROPHETIC POINTS TO REMEMBER

- Throughout history, mountains have been scaled, operas written, monuments built and races won because of friendship.
- What are you doing to advance the Kingdom of God?
- Your uniqueness determines the quality of your calling.
- Your uniqueness determines your level of anointing.
- Your uniqueness determines your results!

Intermedia
Publishing Group

Publishing That Works For You

Do you need a speaker?

Do you want Bishop Robert E. Joyce to speak to your group or event? Then contact Larry Davis at: **(623) 337-8710** or email: **ldavis@intermediapr.com** or use the contact form at: **www.intermediapr.com**.

Whether you want to purchase bulk copies of *The Still Small Voice in the Game of Life* or buy another book for a friend, get it now at: **www.imprbooks.com**.

If you have a book that you would like to publish, contact Terry Whalin, Publisher, at Intermedia Publishing Group, (623) 337-8710 or email: twhalin@intermediapub.com or use the contact form at: www.intermediapub.com.